# Young Offenders and the Law

How does the law deal with young offenders, and to what extent does the law protect and promote the rights of young people in conflict with the law? These are the central issues addressed by *Young Offenders and the Law* in its examination of the legal response to the phenomenon of youth offending, and the contemporary forces that shape the law.

This book develops the reader's understanding of the sociological, criminological, historical, political, and philosophical approaches to youth offending in England and Wales, and also presents a comparative review of developments in other jurisdictions. It provides a comprehensive critical analysis of the legislative and policy framework currently governing the operation of the youth justice system in England and Wales, and evaluates the response of the legal system in light of modern legislative framework and international best practice. All aspects of trial and pre-trial procedure affecting young offenders are covered, including: the age of criminal responsibility, police powers, trial procedure, together with the full range of detention facilities and non-custodial options.

*Young Offenders and the Law* provides, for the first time, a primary source of reference on youth offending. It is an essential text for undergraduate and postgraduate students of Law, Criminology, and Criminal Justice Studies.

**Dr Raymond Arthur** is Senior Lecturer in Law at the School of Social Sciences and Law, Teesside University. His research interests include preventing youth crime, the impact of family life on youth offending, the youth justice system, and child law. Recent publications include *Family Life and Youth Offending: Home is Where the Hurt is* (Routledge, 2007), 'Parental Responsibility Laws' in *Reforming Juvenile Justice* (2009), and 'Protecting the Best Interests of the Child' in the *International Journal of Children's Rights* (2010).

# Young Offenders and the Law

How the law responds to youth offending

**Raymond Arthur**

Routledge
Taylor & Francis Group

LONDON AND NEW YORK

First published 2010
by Routledge
2 Park Square, Milton Park, Abingdon, Oxon OX14 4RN

Simultaneously published in the USA and Canada
by Routledge
270 Madison Ave, New York, NY 10016

*Routledge is an imprint of the Taylor & Francis Group, an informa business*

Typeset in Times New Roman by
Book Now Ltd, London
Printed and bound in Great Britain by
CPI Antony Rowe, Chippenham, Wiltshire

*British Library Cataloguing in Publication Data*
A catalogue record for this book is available from the British Library

*Library of Congress Cataloging in Publication Data*
Arthur, Raymond.
Young offenders and the law : how the law responds to youth
offending / Raymond Arthur.
    p. cm.
1. Juvenile justice, Administration of—England. 2. Juvenile
delinquency—England. I. Title.

KD8471.A96 2010
345.42'08—dc22                                                    2009045150

ISBN: 978–0–415–49661–2 (hbk)
ISBN: 978–0–415–49662–9 (pbk)
ISBN: 978–0–203–87816–3 (ebk)

For Caitlin

# Contents

# Tables

# Preface

The aim of this book is to study the way in which the law responds to youth offending. Youth offending has always been the focus of intense political, media and academic interest and debates. These debates have ensured that the issue of youth offending is rife with competing analyses, ambiguities, controversy and conflict. This book will transcend these debates and focus on examining the legal response to the phenomenon of youth offending and the contemporary forces that shape the law on youth offending.

The central issues this book will examine are: how does the law deal with young offenders and to what extent does the law protect and promote the rights of young people in conflict with the law? Readers will be encouraged to develop an understanding of the sociological, criminological, historical, political, and philosophical approaches to youth offending. While the focus will mostly be upon arrangements in England and Wales, there will also be a comparative review of developments in other jurisdictions.

The book is divided into three distinct sections. Part I provides a broad historical perspective of the response of society and the legal system to young offenders. This is set in a context of changing attitudes towards children and outlines the spectrum of responses, from hanging them, to viewing them as non-responsible social casualties. Part I essentially provides a chronology of the evolution of the youth justice system since the nineteenth century, which is a necessary first step towards a comprehensive review of the modern youth justice system. Part II examines important legal principles that underpin how the criminal justice system responds to young people who engage in offending behaviour. Part II starts with a consideration of the international laws that influence how the English legal system deals with young offenders. Part II then examines the contentious issue of the age at which young people are held criminally responsible for their behaviour, the ancient protection of *doli incapax*, the extent to which the principle of protecting the welfare of the child is still relevant in the modern youth justice system and the current emphasis on youth crime prevention. Part III provides a systematic analysis of the English youth justice system in practice, from the young person's first involvement with the youth justice system, usually with the police, through the various diversionary programmes designed to prevent any further offending, through prosecution and trial, to sentencing and detention. Each chapter ends with a discussion topic and some suggested further reading in order to encourage further reflection and research of the complexity of youth offending and how the legal system responds to this behaviour.

Work on this book began over 10 years ago at the University of Limerick, Ireland. To get it to print would not have been possible without the support and encouragement of family, colleagues and the publishers. I am grateful to Gerhard Boomgaarden, Miranda Thirkettle and Jennifer Dodd at Routledge for their expertise in bringing this book to print. Many thanks to colleagues and students at Teesside University for their scholarly and friendly support and for the many discussions of the issues raised in this book. I am particularly grateful for the support of family and friends. Most importantly, I want to thank Siobhán for all her encouragement, support and affection throughout this long process and to Caitlin, whose arrival in the middle of work on this book has been an enormous source of joy and inspiration.

# Part I

# Historical development of the English youth justice system

# 1    Development of a separate youth justice system – historical perspectives

## Introduction

This chapter will examine how concepts of youth, childhood and adolescence have been developed and how separate systems of justice were established for young people in the nineteenth century. Examining the historical development of the youth justice system will help you to understand that the problem of youth crime is not a recent problem. It also provides a benchmark against which the modern youth justice system can be compared and contrasted.

## Development of childhood

Childhood has not always been a time in the life cycle to which much importance has been attached. During the Middle Ages there was no concept of childhood, youth or adolescence; Aries notes that various languages did not even have words to describe childhood (Aries, 1962: 28–9). Historically there were no games for children; children participated in manual work, drinking alcohol and gambling. Children were legally the property of their parents and were used by them as a vital source of family income and placed in work as soon as they could be economically active. Children below seven years of age were acknowledged as being physically vulnerable, but once the child was older than seven years the child was simply regarded as a small adult. In the Middle Ages child labour from the age of four years was a long established rural practice and apprenticeships often began at the age of seven years. With the arrival of the industrial revolution, the children of the poor formed the bulk of factory labour. Such a situation was considered beneficial to families, in order to maintain a level of income, and also to factory owners who benefited from a source of labour. Such realities were bolstered by law. Compulsory education did not begin to develop until the 1870s and cruelty to children did not become a criminal offence until 1899 with the passing of the Prevention of Cruelty to Children Act 1899. The 1899 Act aimed to deter the mistreatment of children and made it an offence for a person over the age of 16 years to 'assault, ill-treat, neglect or abandon any child for whom he has responsibility'.

The law made no special provisions for young people who committed crime. Provided a child was over the minimum age of criminal responsibility (seven years of age) and had mischievous discretion, the child was as fully liable as an adult to the penalties provided by law. Mischievous discretion means that at the time of the alleged offence the child was aware that what he or she was doing was seriously wrong as opposed to being merely mischievous or naughty. Otherwise there was no special protection for young offenders; once a child was aged seven the child was held responsible for any misdemeanour or crimes they committed. If children were old enough to commit a crime, then they were old enough to be sentenced the same as adults. Children convicted of offences were sentenced the same as adults.

The pre-Norman Laws of Ine dating from the eighth century suggest the age of 10 as the age of criminal responsibility. Bracton explained this by equating a child's 'innocence of purpose' with a 'lack of intention to harm' (Bracton, *c.* 1250). The test was whether the child had the understanding of an adult. By the fifteenth century the pre-Norman age limits had been lowered. Hale, in his seventeenth-century textbook explains the laws incorporation of the distinctions between infancy (up to seven years of age), the age approaching puberty (seven to thirteen years of age), and puberty (over 14 years) (Hale, 1736). Other than this, the criminal law accorded no differentiations in the method of bringing offenders to trial, in the form of the trial itself and in the punishment that could be enforced. Young offenders were liable to the same forms of trial and punishments, including capital conviction, transportation and imprisonment.

## Development of a separate youth justice system

In Victorian times the criminal justice system was very severe. The Victorians believed in institutions: mad-houses for the mad and prisons for the bad. Consequently the legal system did not differentiate on the basis of age. However during the nineteenth century concern developed about the moral contamination of young people. The first public body to investigate youth offending behaviour, established in 1815, was the Society for Investigating the Causes of the Alarming Increase of Juvenile Delinquency in the Metropolis. The Society's evidence was taken from interviewing children already incarcerated in prison. It concluded that the main causes of juvenile offending in England's developing and industrialising capital city were, amongst other things, the improper conduct of parents and the want of education. The causes of crime were found to be firmly rooted in the low moral condition of parents and in parental neglect. This resulted in the emergence of the view that adult and young offenders must be separated in order to avoid the 'contamination' of the younger offenders. Pressure to develop separate institutions for young offenders was also developing from voluntary organisations such as the Philanthropic Society and the Society for the Suppression of Juvenile Vagrancy. The Philanthropic Society was founded in 1788 and aimed to reform the 'depraved' and the 'deprived'. An asylum with no surrounding wall was established in Hackney to provide some resemblance of home for up to 60 children. Each child was assigned to a local manufacturer to provide industrial instruction; daily prayers and church attendance were compulsory. In 1792 further property was acquired complete with its own dormitory and workshops. The distinguishing feature of these institutions was the principle of self-instruction under supervision.

Gradually highly-controlled institutions in which young offenders could be reformed and reclaimed were developed. In 1823 a separate convict prison ship for juveniles was introduced. In 1838 the first penal institution solely for young people was opened at Parkhurst. The opening of Parkhurst was applauded as a means of protecting young prisoners. Parkhurst was designed to segregate young offenders from adult offenders and thus prevent young people from being tainted by adults in prison. However its regime was very repressive: prisoners were manacled and confined to their cells for long periods of time except for brief periods of exercise and religious instruction. The new prison was designed to be 'stern in its aspect, and penal in its character' (Inspector of Prisons, 1836: 98; Inspector of Prisons, 1838: 112–14). The influential philanthropist Mary Carpenter was a forceful critic of penal regimes, such as Parkhurst. She was convinced that reformation depended on meeting the perceived needs of children for care and support as well as overt discipline. She viewed the causes of crime as being rooted in the deficiencies of working-class family life. Carpenter articulated her views to a House of Commons Committee: 'I have great objection to calling them [children] even semi-criminal because the word has a moral meaning. I consider the condition they are in as that of extreme neglect' (cited in Manton, 1976: 14). Carpenter described prisons as the 'most costly, most inefficacious for any end but to prepare the child for a life of crime' (Carpenter, 1853: 13). Carpenter promoted a more child-centred approach to youth offending. Carpenter's views were to gain legal status. She did not believe in allocating specific periods of detention for young offenders; for Carpenter, the goal was 'curing' the young person and cures proceeded at varying paces and thus the period of detention must be indeterminate (Radzinowicz and Hood, 1990: 169).

The Juvenile Offenders Act 1847 was the first statute to distinguish between adults and juvenile offenders. Children under 14 years and accused of theft could be tried summarily, subject to their consent. Instead of committing children to prison to await their trials, summary powers of conviction made the process of trial for children quicker and more private. Cases were heard by magistrates in a court in the district where the offence is alleged to have occurred. The sentencing powers of magistrates were quite limited. Other important developments were the Youthful Offenders

Act 1854 and the Industrial Schools Act 1857. These Acts acknowledged for the first time that youth offending was a distinct social problem and that children who offended lacked full responsibility for their actions. Both of these Acts introduced the concept of reformatory treatment rather than just punishment. Under the 1854 Act the courts were allowed to sentence any child convicted of an offence to a reformatory school for between two and five years, thus replacing prison with institutions designed specifically for children. Reformatory schools were designed to provide industrial training to juvenile offenders. Reformatory schools were managed by voluntary associations under the inspection of state authorities. They were financed by the state and parental contributions: the courts could order the parents of an offender to pay up to five shillings a week for the care and maintenance of the child, all other costs being met by the state. Reformatories reflected Victorian attitudes to 'save' delinquent children from a life of crime. The aim of the Reformatory school was to suppress inappropriate behaviour rigorously but within a family atmosphere suitable for misdirected children (Carlebach, 1970: 72).

Under the 1857 Act children found begging or who had no visible means of subsistence were deemed to be beyond parental control and could be sent to an industrial school indefinitely, though not beyond the age of 15. The purpose of industrial schools was to help vulnerable children before they committed a crime. Industrial schools contrast with reformatory schools in that industrial schools were for potential, rather than actual, offenders. The Report of the Department Committee on Reformatory and Industrial Schools 1896 explained the distinction: '[the] inmates of reformatories are always called youthful offenders, and those of industrial schools always children'. The law believed that parents should not be allowed to bring up their child in a way which would almost ensure that the child would become a criminal. The Amending Act 1861 widened the category of children who could be sent to industrial schools to include children begging, and in the company of thieves. Courts could also use their discretion to send a child under 12 years of age who had committed an offence to an industrial school, if they felt that an industrial school would be more appropriate than a reformatory school. The Consolidation Act 1866 widened the category even further to include orphans and children whose parents were in prison.

The Summary Jurisdiction Act 1879 allowed for all offences committed by children below 12 years of age to be tried summarily, except in the case of homicide. The Reformatory Schools Act 1884 allowed for children between the ages of five and sixteen years to be sent to a reformatory school for two years, however this had to be preceded by two weeks imprisonment in an adult prison. The Youthful Offenders Act 1885 allowed for children to be sent to reform school for between two and five years, preceded by two weeks in prison. The view was that the punishment would not take long, however the reform of the child would take years. This Act also allowed for parents to be ordered to pay for their child's upkeep in reformatory school. The 1855 Act thus represented the first attempt to enforce parental responsibility; this is an issue which will be examined in more detail in Chapter 11. The Probation of First Offenders Act 1887 provided magistrates with the power to release young offenders convicted for the first time of committing a minor offence. However, because no supervision of the young person was required, magistrates did not use this power very much (Morgan, 2007: 203). The 1893 Reformatory Schools Act allowed magistrates to commit offenders to reformatories without the need to send them to prison. The 1899 Reformatory Schools Act abolished the prison element: children could either be sent to prison or reformatory school, but not both.

By the end of the nineteenth century reformatories and industrial schools held more than 30,000 inmates, that is one in every 230 children. However, industrial schools and reformatories were essentially prisons in all but name (Bedingfield, 1998: 462). Also under the 1854 Act magistrates could continue to send juveniles to adult prisons if they so wished. In fact between 1856 and 1875 sentences to reformatory detention formed only 13 per cent of all child commitments to prison. The reformatory school was thus grafted on to the existing institutions of punishment and justice, it did not replace them. Nonetheless it is important to note that, before the reformatory and industrial schools of the 1840s and 1850s, it was impossible to talk with any precision of the existence of young offenders. It was the very existence of the sentencing alternatives of reformatories and industrial schools that enabled juvenile delinquency and young offenders gradually to take on their modern meaning as a clearly identifiable and distinctive social problem.

## Developments in the USA

During the nineteenth century in the United States of America, similar efforts were made to separate adult offenders from young offenders. Reformatory and industrial schools sprang up throughout the USA to provide corrective treatment and refuge for delinquent and neglected children. In the USA there was also a concern that adults and children were separated not just at the custodial stage but also at the trial stage. The first court of law dedicated exclusively to children was founded in Chicago in 1899 and allowed for cases of youth offending to be heard in special courtrooms separate from adult cases. The juvenile court was not a criminal court and the rules of criminal procedure did not apply. This court operated in a highly informal manner; unlike the adult courts, accused youth would not be tried in a formal, open and adversarial process. Instead the court aimed to provide children with care, custody and discipline. Accordingly dispositions were based on an examination of the young persons' circumstances and needs (Morris and Giller, 1987: 11–12). The first juvenile court judge asked 'why is it not the duty of the state, instead of asking merely whether a boy or a girl has committed a specific offence, to find out what he is physically, mentally, morally . . . '(Mack, 1909: 107). Using broad discretion the juvenile court judge was to provide the necessary help and guidance to a young person who might otherwise proceed further down the path of chronic crime (Fox, 1996). The basis of the new juvenile courts was the concept of *parens patriae*. This is derived from the Chancery Courts which were primarily concerned with protecting property rights, but in this context the concept of *parens patriae* was developed to encompass the responsibility of the state to act in the best interests of the child (Morris and Giller, 1987: 12). In England for many centuries the Chancery Courts recognised the duty of the Crown to look after the prop-

Table 1.1  Important dates in the development of the youth justice system, 1788–1899

| | |
|---|---|
| 1788 | Foundation of the Philanthropic Society to care for and treat vagrant children. |
| 1816 | Publication of the report of the Society for Investigating the Causes of the Alarming Increase of Juvenile Delinquency in the Metropolis. |
| 1835 | Mary Carpenter founded the Working & Visiting Society. |
| 1838 | The first separate state institution (Parkhurst Prison) for young offenders is established. |
| 1847 | Juvenile Offender Act 1847 – children under 14 to be tried summarily by magistrates and be subject to less severe punishments. |
| 1854 | Youthful Offenders Act 1854 – any child convicted of an offence could be sentenced to a reformatory school for between two and five years. |
| 1857 | Industrial Schools Act 1857 – children deemed to be beyond parental control could be sent indefinitely to an industrial school. |
| 1861 | The Amending Act 1861 widened the category of children who could be sent to industrial schools to include children begging and in the company of thieves. |
| 1866 | The Consolidation Act 1866 widened the category even further to include orphans and children whose parents were in prison. |
| 1879 | The Summary Jurisdiction Act 1879 allowed for all offences committed by children below 12 years of age to be tried summarily, except in the case of homicide. |
| 1884 | The Reformatory Schools Act 1884 allowed for children between the ages of five and sixteen years to be sent to a reformatory school for two years, preceded by two weeks imprisonment in an adult prison. |
| 1885 | The Youthful Offenders Act 1885 allowed for children to be sent to reform school for between two and five years, preceded by two weeks in prison. |
| 1887 | The Probation of First Offenders Act 1887 provided magistrates with the power to release first time young offenders convicted of committing a minor offence. |
| 1893 | The Reformatory Schools Act 1893 allowed magistrates to commit offenders to reformatories without the need to send them to prison. |
| 1899 | The Reformatory Schools Act 1899 abolished the prison element, children could either be sent to prison or reformatory. Prevention of Cruelty to Children Act 1899 – law preventing cruelty to children. The first youth court was opened in Chicago. |

erty of lunatics and children. Traditionally the Chancery Court would manage the estate of children whose parents had died until the child was 21 years old, thus setting a legal precedent for court intervention in the lives of children. Accordingly the US juvenile court applied the principle of *parens patriae* to dealing with young offenders and considered that the young offender lacked proper parental care, not because their parents had died, but because their parents were weak or criminal (Weijers, 1999: 335). Acting in its role as *parens patriae*, the US juvenile court could take children out of their homes and place them in a reform school without their parents having any say in the matter. By 1920 all but three states in the USA would have a separate juvenile court.

---

### Discussion topic

How have concerns about children's welfare influenced the development of official recognition that young offenders should be treated differently from adult offenders?

---

### *Comment*

The process of distinguishing both a period of childhood, and a morality of childhood, began in the late Middle Ages. During the nineteenth century through a combination of legislation and institutional projects, voluntary initiatives, imprisonment and cultural concepts the unique needs of the young began to be recognised. The invention of the 'neglected child' led inevitably to the invention of the 'juvenile delinquent'. As the prominent child welfare activist and Chief of the US Federal Children's Bureau wrote in 1898: 'if the child is the material out of which men and women are made, the neglected child is the material out of which paupers and criminals are made' (quoted in Mennell, 1973). During this period special emphasis was placed upon separating adult and young offenders in order to avoid the moral contamination of the younger offenders. Gradually this led to the establishment of separate, highly-controlled institutions in which young offenders could be reformed and reclaimed. From these humble origins emerged the modern youth justice system which will be examined in the next chapter.

### Suggested further reading

Hendrick, H. (2002) 'Constructions and reconstructions of British childhood: an interpretative survey, 1800 to the present' in Muncie, J., Hughes, G. and McLaughlin, E. (eds) *Youth Justice Critical Readings*, London: Sage, pp. 22–8.

May, M. (2002) 'Innocence and experience: the evolution of the concept of juvenile delinquency in the mid-nineteenth century' in Muncie, J., Hughes, G. and McLaughlin, E. (eds) *Youth Justice Critical Readings*, London: Sage, pp. 98–112.

Morris, A. and Giller, H. (1987) *Understanding Juvenile Justice*, London: Croom Helm, pp. 3–36.

# 2 Development of the youth justice system – 1900–69

## Introduction

Chapter 2 will examine the development of the youth justice system through the major part of the twentieth century, up to 1969. Chapter 3 will examine the period from 1969 to the present. Chapter 2 will examine the conflict between legalism and welfarism. This chapter will establish that the principle that children and young people should be protected from the full weight of adult criminal justice systems underpins the concept of 'welfare' in youth justice, and can be traced back to the invention of juvenile delinquency in the early nineteenth century and the subsequent inception of specific legislation, court structures, policies, procedures and practices for the processing of young offenders at the beginning of the twentieth century.

## Development of a separate court in England for young people who offend

The Youthful Offenders Act 1901 extended the use of alternatives to prison for young people and also made parents liable for the behaviour of their children. Section 4 of the 1901 Act allowed magistrates to remand young people accused of a crime to a workhouse or the custody of any fit person who was willing to receive him instead of prison. The 1901 Act also allowed the courts to order parents of young offenders (under 16 years of age) to pay whatever costs or compensation as the court considered reasonable. The Probation Act 1907 extended the use of alternatives to prison. The 1907 Act put probation on a statutory footing which allowed courts to appoint probation officers and children's probation officers for cases involving young people below 16 years of age (section 3, Probation Act 1907). The 1907 Act introduced the probation order which required probation officers to 'advise, assist and befriend' the young person towards rehabilitation. The effect of the 1901 Act and the 1907 Act was to develop supervised probation as a widely used penalty.

The Prevention of Crime Act 1908 created a new specialist detention centre for young people – the borstal. Young offenders, between the ages of

16 and 21, could be sentenced to a borstal for a period of between one and three years. Section 2 allowed the court to transfer from a reformatory school to a borstal any young offender who had breached the rules of the reformatory or escaped from the reformatory. Borstal training involved a regime of hard physical work, technical and educational instruction, character formation, respect for authority and a strong moral atmosphere. A young person in borstal would work through a series of grades based on privileges.

The Children Act 1908 created a separate and distinct system of justice for children based on the juvenile court. The 1908 Act established juvenile courts with both civil jurisdiction over children in need and criminal jurisdiction over offending children. The 1908 Act assumed that children were less responsible than adults for their actions and should not be subject to the full rigours of the criminal law. The 1908 Act represented the first time in England that a statute recognised the principle that juvenile offenders should be heard separately from adult offenders in special sittings of the magistrates' court. With the exception of murder, the juvenile court had the power to deal with all offences committed by young people aged between seven and seventeen years. The courts also had jurisdiction over young people in need of care. Juvenile courts were required to sit at different times and in a different place from adult courts and the public were excluded from the proceedings of the juvenile court. The press were not excluded, but newspaper reporters were asked not to publish children's names and addresses. The main sentencing options available to the juvenile court were discharge, discharge to the supervision of a probation officer, committal to the care of a relative or other fit person, committal to a reformatory or industrial school, whipping, payment of a fine and imprisonment if the juvenile was over 14 and could not be held anywhere else. Specifically excluded from the jurisdiction of the juvenile court were children charged jointly with an adult, children charged with murder, attempted murder, manslaughter and wounding with intent. Such children were to be tried and sentenced in an adult court. The Children Act 1908 abolished the death penalty for children below 16 years of age. The 1908 Act also prevented magistrates from sentencing children under 14 years to prison and those between 14 and 15 years could only be sent to prison if the court determined that the children were 'unruly'. Sir Evely Ruggles-Brise, Chairman of the Prison Commission hailed the Children Act 1908 in the following terms:

> The passing of the Children's Act, 1908, which practically forbids imprisonment before 16 years of age, marks the last stage in that slow and tedious journey which had to be undertaken by many devoted men and women who were conscious of the grave evils resulting from imprisonment, before it was generally realized that it was not by throwing children and young persons automatically and indiscriminately into gaol, that the grave problem of juvenile delinquency was going to be solved.
>
> (Ruggles-Brise, 1921: 101)

The new juvenile courts functioned in much the same way as the adult courts did. Although the courts were given a wide range of flexible dispositions, decisions were governed by considerations such as the seriousness of the offence and the interest of the public (Morris and Giller, 1987: 11). The English juvenile court viewed the juvenile as a miniature adult who had to be protected by the due process of law and its accompanying procedures and safeguards (Morris and Giller, 1987: 67). Not until the Children and Young Persons Act 1933 was it required that magistrates sitting in the juvenile court be specifically selected for this task, that the court act *in loco parentis*, and have regard to 'the welfare of the child'. The term *in loco parentis* means that the court can act as a substitute parent for the child.

## Young offenders – children in need of care or punishment?

By the early twentieth century the use of industrial schools was in decline. This was partly due to the First World War: lots of young people had been sent to the trenches. Between the two World Wars there was a lot of sympathy towards young people, possibly due to a whole generation of young people being killed. The 1927 Moloney Committee recommended that welfare principles should dominate the youth justice system. In 1927 the Moloney Committee recognised the importance of the welfare of young offenders, most of whom were victims of social and psychological conditions and in need of individualised treatment (Home Office, 1927). In this respect the Committee felt that there was little to distinguish the young offender from the neglected child:

> It is often a mere accident whether he is brought before the court because he was wandering or beyond control or because he committed some offence. Neglect leads to delinquency.
>
> (Home Office, 1927: 6)

The Moloney Committee recommended the development of a juvenile court especially adapted for young people which was staffed with people chosen on account of their special qualifications: those with 'a love of young people, sympathy with their interests, and an imaginative insight into their differences' (Home Office, 1927: 25). The Moloney Committee also recommended that the duty of the court was not to punish the young person but to readjust and rehabilitate the young person. Thus the Committee recommended that juvenile court magistrates should have the fullest possible information about young people appearing before them, including information about their home circumstances, school performance and medical report.

The recommendations of the Moloney Committee formed the basis of the Children and Young Persons Act 1933. Section 44 of the Children and Young Persons Act 1933 imposes an important welfare principle which requires every court to have regard to the welfare of a child or young person who is brought before it, either as an offender or otherwise. The welfare principle's main virtue is that it requires a decision made with respect to a child to be justified from the point of view of a judgment about the child's interests. It would be inconsistent with the welfare principle to make a decision that is overtly justified by reference to the way the outcome benefited some other interests (Eekelaar, 2002). The Children and Young Persons Act 1933 amalgamated industrial schools and reformatories into 'approved schools'. The 1933 Act allowed for offenders and non-offenders to be sent to approved schools for up to 3 years. Offenders and non-offenders were being sent to the same places where the regime was aimed at education and discipline, rather than punishment. Thus non-offenders became tarred with the same brush as offenders. The 1933 Act prohibited capital punishment for those under the age of 18 years and created remand homes to accommodate remanded young people separate from adult offenders. The 1933 Act also required juvenile court magistrates to have special qualifications for their work in the juvenile courts. However, in practice, the courts remained criminal courts.

After the Second World War there was a rise in juvenile crime associated with the social disorganisation of post-war Britain. Again, it was believed that the problem could be solved by the welfare state. This was the background to the Curtis Committee. In 1946, almost twenty years after the Moloney Committee, the Curtis Committee reported on the existing models of provision for children who were deprived of a 'normal' home life (Home Office, 1946). While deprived children were the focus of the Curtis Report, the Committee noted that deprived children and young offenders were both victims of family and environmental circumstances that triggered emotional disturbance. Following the report of the Curtis Committee, the Children Act 1948 set up local authority children's departments to provide for the first time a specialised and individualised social work service to meet the needs of young people. The justification for extending the state's right to intervene was the belief that the roots of young people's problems were in 'the malfunctioning of individuals and their faulty upbringing'. The formal duty of local authorities to 'set to work' the children of the poor was replaced with the duty to 'further his best interests, and to afford him opportunity for the proper development of his character and abilities' (section 12, Children Act 1948), thus blurring the distinction between young offenders and children in need of protection.

The Criminal Justice Act 1948 abolished corporal punishment as a sentence and also abolished imprisonment for those under 17 years of age. The 1948 Act introduced two new dispositions – detention centres for those aged between 14 and 17 years and attendance centres for those aged between 8 and 17 years. Detention centres were introduced for those who did not require long term training in an approved school or borstal, but for whom non-custodial measures were inappropriate (Morris and Giller, 1987: 72).

The detention centre reflected the belief that young people would respond to strict discipline, but it also incorporated elements of training. Attendance centres were intended to punish young people by depriving them of their leisure time. The centres were likened to school detention for behaviour which went 'not much beyond a schoolboy's disobedience' (McClintock, 1963: 6). Section 19 of the Criminal Justice Act 1948 excluded boys who had previously been in a borstal, detention centre or approved school. It was in relation to attendance centres that the phrase 'short and sharp punishment' was coined by Lord Templewood during the debates on the Criminal Justice Bill (Templewood, 1948). Both the Children Act 1948 and the Criminal Justice Act 1948 reflect ambivalence towards young people in trouble. The need to care for those seen as victims is balanced by the need to discipline those seen as bad (Morris and Giller, 1987: 73).

The Ingleby Committee also accepted the view that the needs of the neglected child and the young offender were the same, both being a product of 'family failure'. The Ingleby Committee was set up in 1956 to look into the operation of the juvenile court and consider what new powers and duties could be given to local authorities to prevent the neglect of children at home (Home Office, 1960). The Ingleby Committee recommended the retention of the juvenile court and suggested raising the age of criminal responsibility from eight to twelve years, with the possibility of it becoming 13 or 14 years. Because few of the recommendations of the Ingleby Committee were incorporated into the Children and Young Persons Act 1963, the 1963 Act was quite a limited measure. Nonetheless it raised the age of criminal responsibility from eight to ten years and expanded the category of 'in need of care and protection' to that of being 'in need of care, protection and control'. Local authorities were also given the duty to engage in preventive work with children and families thought to be 'at risk'. Whereas the Children Act 1948 had given social workers the task of rescuing children by taking them into care, the 1963 Act was more ambitious in that it sought to prevent trouble before it developed.

The Children and Young Persons Act 1969 was underpinned by a philosophy of treatment which removed any lingering distinction between children who offended and those who needed care and protection. The causes of offending and deprivation were seen as the same, both types of children suffered from essentially the same problems and had the same treatment needs. This Act advocated a rise in the age of criminal responsibility and sought alternatives to detention by way of treatment, non-criminal care proceedings and care orders. The 1969 Act advocated a range of interventions intended to deal with young offenders through systems of supervision, treatment and social welfare in the community rather than punishment in custodial institutions. It was quite explicitly based on a social welfare approach to young offenders. Authority and discretion were shifted out of the hands of the police, magistrates and prisons, and into the hands of the local authorities, social workers and Department of Health. For example, section 1(2) of the 1969 Act provided that one reason justifying a civil care order or a supervision order was that the young person was guilty of any offence, excluding homicide. It also had to be proved that there was a need for care and control which the young offender was unlikely to receive unless a court order were made. The separate power to commit a child to care in criminal proceeding (section 7(7) Children and Young Persons Act 1969) also reflected a fundamental purpose in the legislation, which was to treat all children in trouble as children in need of care and protection. The effect of these provisions was to explicitly acknowledge that committing an offence could be a symptom of social need. The 1969 Act gave primacy to the family and the social circumstances of the deprived and underprivileged; it aimed to reduce the criminalisation of young people and to increase the support and care available to them. Also it raised the age of criminal responsibility to 14 years of age. The 1969 Act effectively legislated to abolish prosecuting any child under 14 years of age for any criminal offence except homicide. Those aged between 14 and 16 years of age could still have been prosecuted, but non-criminal care proceedings would be available to deal with these young people.

Many European countries were adopting a similar approach to the Children and Young Persons Act 1969 at this time. For example, Belgium passed the Youth Protection Act 1965 which allowed for children in danger and delinquent children to be considered as a single category and dealt with using a child welfare orientation that decriminalised the delinquent behaviour of young people. At the same time, in Scotland, the Kilbrandon Committee believed that, in terms of the child's actual needs, the legal distinction between young offenders and children in need of care or protection was very often of little practical significance (Kilbrandon, 1964). Kilbrandon argued that more often than not the problems of the child in need and the delinquent child can be traced to shortcomings in the normal upbringing process in either the home, the family environment or in the schools. Kilbrandon described such children, whether they were children in need or offenders, as 'hostages to fortune'. It was considered essential to extend to this minority of children the measures that their needs dictate and of which they have previously been deprived. The views expressed by Kilbrandon formed the basis of the Social Work (Scotland) Act 1968, now incorporated in the Children (Scotland) Act 1995. The Scottish approach is to treat children in trouble with the law as children in need of care and protection. The Scottish system of responding to youth offending will be considered in more detail in Chapter 6.

Although the English Children and Young Persons Act 1969 aimed to reduce the criminalisation of young people and to increase the support and care available to them, it did not have an easy passage through Parliament. Conservative party politicians argued that it was unjust, that it gave insufficient recognition to the constructive role of the juvenile court, and that it interfered with police work with young people, especially in regard to more serious offences (Bottoms, 1974). The Magistrates Association was also opposed to the Children and Young Persons Act 1969 blaming it for the vast increases in youth crime (Berlino and Wansell, 1974), thus precipitating a moral panic about the powerlessness of the juvenile court. Following the defeat of the Wilson government in the 1970 general election, the incoming Heath administration was no more inclined to implement the provisions of the 1969 Act when in government than it had been to support them in opposition. Consequently large sections of the 1969 Act were never implemented and the social welfare ideology underlying the Act never came to fruition. The new Conservative party government elected in 1970 declared that it would not implement those sections of the Act that were intended to raise the age of criminal responsibility from 10 to 14 and to replace criminal proceedings with care proceedings. Essentially the Conservative party government objected to state intervention in criminal matters through a welfare rather than a judicial body. Similarly magistrates and the police responded to the undermining of their key positions in the justice system by becoming more punitively minded and declining the opportunity to use community sentences on a large scale. Consequently juvenile courts continued to function largely as they had before and, though care proceedings following commission of an offence were made possible, such powers were used sparingly (Cavadino and Dignan, 1992; Newburn, 1997; Rutter and Giller, 1983). Rather than replacing the old structures of youth justice, the new welfare principles were simply grafted onto them. Care proceedings were made in criminal cases but it was still possible to

*Table 2.1* Important dates in the development of the youth justice system, 1900–69

| | |
|---|---|
| 1901 | The Youthful Offenders Act 1901 extended the use of alternatives to prison for young people and also made parents liable for the behaviour of their children. |
| 1907 | The Probation Act 1907 extended the use of alternatives to prison. |
| 1908 | The Prevention of Crime Act 1908 created the borstal. |
| | The Children Act 1908 created a separate and distinct system of justice for children based on the juvenile court. |
| 1933 | The Children and Young Persons Act 1933 requires every court to have regard to the welfare of a child or young person who is brought before it. |
| 1948 | The Children Act 1948 set up local authority children's departments to provide a specialised and individualised social work service to meet the needs of young people. |
| | The Criminal Justice Act 1948 introduced detention centres for those aged between 14 and 17 years and attendance centres for those aged between 8 and 17 years. |
| 1963 | The Children and Young Persons Act 1963 raised the age of criminal responsibility from 8 to 10 years. |
| 1969 | The Children and Young Persons Act 1969 advocated a range of interventions intended to deal with young offenders through systems of supervision, treatment and social welfare in the community rather than punishment in custodial institutions. |

take criminal proceedings against children under 14 years of age. Care proceedings were very rarely used, and were largely targeted at young women on the grounds of moral danger and for status offences such as running away from home and staying out late at night, which would not be punishable by law if committed by an adult and rarely considered as serious if committed by boys.

The issue of providing welfare and justice for children and young people remains vexed. Both can be pursued for progressive or reactionary reasons, as means through which youth can be protected from the rigours of the adult system of justice but also made to endure more punitive forms of intervention. The twentieth century was marked by a conflict between welfarism and legalism. Wefarism recommended addressing the child's needs irrespective of offending behaviour whereas legalism (or justice) recommended using legally-sanctioned force which was proportionate to the child's offence and premised on what the child had done.

---

### Discussion topic

Explain the characteristic features of a 'welfare' approach to children in trouble with the law and examine any problems this approach may pose.

---

*Comment*

The welfare approach reached its peak in England with the passing of the Children and Young Persons Act 1969, its core idea being that young offenders were not that different from young people in other kinds of trouble and that they should not experience the full force of the prosecution system unless all other available avenues have been exhausted. Youths were to be handled by civil care proceedings and the incarceration of young people was to be discouraged. This welfare approach was to disappear in the following decades.

The welfare approach is based on the idea that experts can assess the needs of children, carry out a programme of resocialisation, and end up with a healthy law-abiding citizen who was rehabilitated, individually deterred, but not necessarily punished. This approach relies on the assumption that it is possible and necessary to discover the needs of the child and social workers are the people to do this. Ideas about children's development are not scientific, they are moral and value laden and change according to social conditions. Why do we think that doctors/scientists/social workers know about children in general and particular children? Children as a group do not have the backing of powerful groups within society to have their needs taken into account.

## Suggested further reading

Bedingfield, D. (1998) *The Child in Need: Children, The State and the Law*, Bristol: Family Law, pp. 460–72.

Bottoms, A. (2002) 'On the decriminalization of English juvenile courts' in Muncie, J., Hughes, G. and McLaughlin, E. (eds) *Youth Justice Critical Readings*, London: Sage, pp. 216–27.

Hendrick, H. (2006) 'Histories of Youth Crime and Justice' in Goldson, B. and Muncie, J. (eds) *Youth Crime and Justice*, London: Sage, pp. 3–16.

# 3   The youth justice system – from the Children and Young Persons Act 1969 to the present

## Introduction

Chapter 3 will examine the development of the youth justice system from the end of the twentieth century to the present day. Chapter 3 will examine the youth justice system during the 1980s when law and policy encouraged diverting young people from court and from custody, with the result that the proportion of young offenders in custody decreased dramatically. This chapter will examine how and why this approach to youth offending changed dramatically during the 1990s. From the mid-1990s youth justice law and policy became focussed on a punitive response to young people's behaviour. Chapter 3 will examine how this change has influenced and shaped the current youth justice system.

## Protecting the legal rights of young offenders – the 1980s

The Criminal Justice Act 1982 reflected the general agreement in the 1980s that changes were needed to reverse the unintended consequences of the 1969 Act and take growing account of the concerns for justice and the rights of children. The view emerged that if you were going to interfere with children's liberty it should be done in a legal arena and children's rights should be protected. Children should be entitled to the same legal protection as adults. This was fuelled by the report of the US President's Commission on Law Enforcement and Administration of Justice and the landmark US court decision *re Gault* (387 US 1 (1967)). The report of the President's Commission on Law Enforcement and Administration of Justice stated that 'the juvenile court is a court of law, charged like other agencies of criminal justice with protecting the community against threatening conduct' (United States Government, 1967). In *re Gault* the Supreme Court ruled that where a young person faced incarceration the young person should be entitled to the protection of due process of law, in the same way as adults. Any period spent in an institution should be proportionate to the offence. This is contrary to the welfare model where you look to the child's needs and keep the child in care for as long as needs be, despite the potential for disproportionate incarceration. The United States Supreme Court condemned a system whereby young people could be subjected to long periods of detention in various forms of institutions without rights to due process, such as the right to counsel, rights against self-incrimination and other procedural protections automatically accorded to adult defendants in criminal trials. The Supreme Court held that due process of law is the primary and indispensable foundation of individual freedom. *Gault* also highlighted a second failing of the welfare approach, namely the lack of proportionality and the potential for indeterminacy in disposals. The United States Supreme Court believed that an individualised welfare approach could lead to indeterminate sentences in the name of treatment, in circumstances where, if an adult had committed the offences, they would have been treated more leniently.

In England and Wales the Criminal Justice Act 1982 aimed to provide the juvenile courts with more flexible and effective powers for dealing with young offenders. The 1982 Act made available to the juvenile courts three new powers of disposal – youth custody, care orders with charge and control conditions, and community service. The 1982 Act required that legal representation be offered to the young person and that social inquiry reports be presented to assist the court, and required that sanctions be determinate and proportionate. The 1982 Act abolished borstals but replaced them with youth custody centres where the sentence was fixed by the courts and not by social workers. The 1982 Act expanded the use of detention centres and empowered the courts to incarcerate young offenders for periods exceeding three years. However the 1982 Act also represented a trend towards looking to alternatives to incarceration for young offenders. The Act embraced the idea of 'intermediate treatment' for offenders aged 17–21 years, effectively raising the age limit of supervision orders made in juvenile courts for young people aged 10–16 years. The 1982 Act provided that no court should impose any custodial sentence on a person aged under 21 years unless the court was satisfied that no other sentence was appropriate because: the offender had demonstrated that they were unable or unwilling to respond to non-custodial methods of treatment; or because a custodial sentence was necessary for the protection of the public; or the offence was so serious that a non-custodial option could not be justified (section 1(4) Criminal Justice Act 1982). This trend towards diversion, decriminalisation and decarceration is also reflected in the Criminal Justice Act 1988 which made theft of an automobile a summary offence, therefore making it more difficult to impose custodial sentences on young offenders, and the Criminal Justice Act 1991 which excluded 14 year olds from youth custody and transferred 17-year-old defendants to the juvenile court. The Criminal Justice Act 1988 also introduced young offender institutions which replaced the youth custody centres introduced in 1982.

The Children Act 1989 removed from the juvenile court the power to order a young person into the care of a local authority (sections 90(1) and (2) Children Act 1989). Care and supervision orders can now only be made in the Family Proceedings Court and only when it is proved that the child in question 'is suffering significant harm' and is 'beyond parental control'. Section 31 of the Children Act 1989 ensured that juvenile courts could no longer make care or supervision orders, these orders could only be made by the Family Proceedings Courts, which was a separate court for civil matters. Thus the 1989 Act represents a complete separation of the child in need and the delinquent child. The Criminal Justice Act 1991 created a new youth court and extended its jurisdiction to young people under 18 years of age. The 1991 Act promoted an approach where no account was taken of personal circumstances or prior criminality. The Act established clear demarcations between serious offences such as violence and burglary and lesser offences which could be dealt with by using community sanctions. The 1991 Act aimed to place less emphasis on custodial measures, reflecting the government's concern about the cost and effectiveness of custody, the government believing that custody is 'an expensive way of making bad people worse' (Home Office, 1990: 27). The main features of the 1991 Act include: an expansion in the upper age limit in the youth court to include 17 year olds; a reduction in the maximum custodial sentence in a young offender institution to 12 months (excluding very serious offences which are covered by section 53 of the Children and Young Persons Act 1933); a raising of the minimum age that a young person can be sentenced to a custodial sentence to 15 years; and the expansion of community sentences for 16 and 17 year olds.

In February 1993 two 10-year-old boys – Robert Thompson and Jon Venables – killed the toddler Jamie Bulger. The then Prime Minister, John Major, declared that 'society needs to condemn a little more and understand a little less' (Major, 1993). The significance of John Major's statement was profound in signalling the shape that subsequent developments in policy and legislation would take. This harsh stance set the tone for refocusing policy and practice, in relation to children in trouble, upon punishment, retribution and the wholesale incarceration of children. The government started to take a tough new stand against young offenders where retribution became the dominant theme resulting in harsher sentences, longer sentences and a philosophy that prison works. The Criminal Justice Act 1993 reinstated the power of the youth court to take account of offenders' previous criminal records, also offences committed while on bail were to be treated as aggravating factors when determining sentences. The Criminal Justice and Public Order Act 1994 lowered the age at which children could be detained in custody for grave crimes such as manslaughter or other crimes of violence from 14 to 10 years of age. The 1994 Act also introduced a range of new measures which extended the courts' remand and sentencing powers to younger offenders by increasing the maximum length of detention in a young offender institution from 12–24 months for 15–17 year olds, allowing the court to remand 12–14 year olds and by introducing secure training orders for 12–14 year old persistent offenders for up to two years, with half being served in a Secure Training Centre. Secure Training Centres are purpose-built centres for young offenders up to the age of 17 years. They are intended to house vulnerable young people in a secure environment where they can be educated and rehabilitated. They are however part of the prison estate.

## The advent of the New Labour government in 1997

In 1996 the Audit Commission report *Misspent Youth* was highly critical of the youth justice system in England and Wales. It concluded that:

> The current system for dealing with youth crime is inefficient and expensive while little is being done to deal effectively with juvenile nuisance. The present arrangements are failing young people who are not being guided away from offending to constructive activities.
>
> (Audit Commission, 1996: 96)

The Audit Commission is an independent body responsible for ensuring that public money is used efficiently, economically and effectively. The New Labour government responded to the Audit Commission's verdict on the youth justice system in the Consultation Paper *No More Excuses – A New Approach to Tackling Youth Crime in England and Wales* in which it suggested that up until 1997 youth offending had been greeted with excuses instead of action (Home Office, 1997a: 1). *No More Excuses* proposed a 'root and branch' overhaul of the youth justice system and a breaking with the philosophy of the 1969 Act (Home Office, 1997a: 9.2). The Crime and Disorder Act 1998 was passed largely without revision following *No More Excuses*. The 1998 Act represents a 'melting pot of principles and ideologies' mixing 'punishment and welfare approaches' perpetuating the confusion over these incompatible frameworks for intervention (Fionda, 1999). Section 37 of the Act establishes preventing offending by children and young people as the principal aim of the youth justice system. It also places all those working in the youth justice system under a duty to have regard to that aim in carrying out their duties. To help deliver this aim the government identified six key objectives for the reformed youth justice system:

1   Tackling delays – halving the time from arrest to sentence for persistent young offenders;
2   Confronting young offenders with the consequences of their offending and assisting them to develop a sense of personal responsibility;
3   Intervening to tackle the known risk factors associated with youth offending, including personal, family, social, educational and health factors;
4   Providing the courts with a range of new penalties appropriate to the seriousness and persistence of offending;

5    Encouraging reparation to the victims by the young offender;
6    Reinforcing the responsibilities of parents.

In order to achieve these objectives the Crime and Disorder Act established six key themes:

(1)   *Partnership and multi-agency work*: sections 6 and 7 of the Crime and Disorder Act encourage the development of local partnerships to provide a local framework and strategy for identifying crime and disorder problems within a particular locality and to provide a response. The principle of inter-agency cooperation is also reaffirmed in section 37 of the Crime and Disorder Act 1998, which places all those carrying out functions in relation to the youth justice system under a statutory duty to have regard to the new principal aim of preventing offending by children and young people. Paragraph 4 of the 'framework document' for the Crime and Disorder Act 1998 explains the incorporation into statute of this aim; it argues that the youth justice system has for 'too long been seen to be separate from wider youth crime prevention work' and that the new statutory aim makes clear the 'important link that there should be between the work of the youth justice system and wider work to help prevent children and young people offending' (Home Office, 1998a). The Crime and Disorder Act places a statutory duty on all local authorities, police forces, police authorities, health authorities and local probation committees to work together in combating problems of crime and disorder in their locality (section 5 Crime and Disorder Act 1998), to secure that, to such extent as is appropriate for their area, all youth justice services are available there (section 38 Crime and Disorder Act 1998), and to ensure that a youth offending team is in place (section 40 Crime and Disorder Act 1998). The youth offending team (YOT) comprises representatives from the police, probation, education and health authorities and the local authority, thus guaranteeing that teams of trained professionals with specific disciplines work together to tackle youth offending. The YOT works with young people aged 10–17 who are offending or at risk of offending, as well as those under 10 in order to prevent offending. The YOT has primary responsibility for coordinating youth justice services across a geographical area, providing a multi-agency service for children and young people at risk of offending, or who are involved in offending behaviour, and carrying out such functions as are assigned to them in the Youth Justice Plan formulated by the local authority (section 41 Crime and Disorder Act 1998). The YOTs aim to deliver a wide range of programmes that tackle offending behaviour at the different stages of its development. YOTs have taken the lead in creating schemes to provide purposeful and engaging activities for young people at risk of offending.

Youth offending teams are also required to coordinate the provision of youth justice services for those in the area who need them (section 38(4)

Crime and Disorder Act 1998). This includes the provision of appropriate adult services under the Crime and Disorder Act final warning scheme provisions (section 65 Crime and Disorder Act 1998); assessment and intervention work in support of final warnings given by the police to young people who admit offending; the prompt provision of pre-sentence reports required by courts in criminal proceedings against young people; participation on youth offender panels; preparation of youth offender contracts; supervision of young people sentenced to a court order; coordination and provision of effective support for young people on bail, through care and post-release supervision for young people sentenced to a detention and training order or other custodial sentence. The Crime and Disorder Act 1998 places a duty on local authorities to formulate and implement annual youth justice plans in consultation with senior officers of the agencies that make up YOTs. Thus much of the youth offending teams core work is with known offenders as well as being involved in preventing offending by young people who have not yet committed offences (Home Office *et al.*, 1998: 32).

(2) *Early intervention and tackling offending behaviour*: this theme is promoted through a range of new orders such as child safety orders (section 11 Crime and Disorder Act 1998), local child curfews (section 14 1998 Act), final warnings (section 65 1998 Act) and more recently with the youth rehabilitation orders (section 1 Criminal Justice and Immigration Act 2008). The child safety order places the child under the supervision of a responsible officer (either a social worker from a local authority social services department or a member of a youth offending team) and requires the child to comply with such requirements as are considered desirable in the interest of securing that the child receives appropriate care, protection and support. A child curfew scheme creates a ban on all children under the age of 10 years being in a public place within a specified area during specified hours and otherwise than under the effective control of a responsible person aged 18 or over. Sections 48 and 49 of the Criminal Justice and Police Act 2001 raise the age limit of child curfew schemes to cover unsupervised children up to and including the age of 15 years. The Crime and Disorder Act scrapped the system of informal and formal cautions and replaced it with 'reprimands' and 'final warnings'. The final warning scheme involves immediate assessment and intervention in order to 'nip offending in the bud'. Section 65 of the Crime and Disorder Act 1998 provides that a police officer can respond to a young person's first offence with a final warning depending on its seriousness. When a final warning is administered, the police officer is required to refer the young person to the local youth offending team for 'assessment'. The youth rehabilitation order (YRO) is the new generic community sentence for young offenders and combines a number of existing community sentences into one generic sentence. It will be the standard community sentence used for the majority of children and young people who offend. The YRO represents a more individualised risk- and needs-based approach

to community sentencing, enabling greater choice from a 'menu' of require-ments. It aims to simplify sentencing for young people, while improving the flexibility of interventions.

(3)    *Reparation*: section 67 of the 1998 Act established the reparation order which is designed to encourage the young offender to acknowledge the consequences of their behaviour. The court can order the young person to make reparation to the victim of the crime or to the local community. The Youth Justice and Criminal Evidence Act 1999 introduced the referral order as a new primary sentencing disposal for 10–17 year olds pleading guilty and convicted for the first time. The disposal involves referring the young offender to a youth offender panel (YOP). The youth offender panel includes lay members from the community and one member of a local youth offending team. The YOP provides a forum where the young offender, members of his family and, if appropriate, the victim can consider the circumstances surrounding the offence and the effect on the victim. The youth offender panel then establishes a 'programme of behaviour' with the young offender to address his offending behaviour which the child will be obliged to observe. The programme of behaviour can include: financial or other reparation to the victim; mediation with the victim; unpaid work or service in the community; attendance at school, educational establishment or work; participation in specified activities such as alcohol or drug treat-ment, counselling, courses addressing offending behaviour; or education or training. The principal aim of the programme of behaviour is the prevention of reoffending by the child. Part III of the Powers of Criminal Courts (Sentencing) Act 2000 provides that the referral order is the standard sentence imposed by the youth courts, or other magistrate court, for all first time offenders under the age of 18 years unless their offending is so serious that it warrants custody or the court orders an absolute discharge or makes a hospital order.

(4)    *Parenting*: the Crime and Disorder Act 1998 reinforces the principle of parental responsibility by introducing the 'parenting order' enabling the court to require the parent of every convicted young offender to attend parenting programmes and if necessary to control the future behaviour of the juvenile in a specified manner. The parenting programmes deal with issues such as experiences of parenting, communication and negotiation skills, parenting style and the importance of consistency, praise and rewards and can include a residential element.

(5)    *More effective custodial sentences*: section 73 of the 1998 Act estab-lished the detention and training order as a new generic custodial sentence. The detention and training order amalgamates the secure training orders for 12–14 year olds with the existing detention in a young offender institu-tion for 15–17 year olds. The detention and training order can be given to

any young offender between the ages of 12 and 17 years and can last from between four months to two years. The first half of the sentence is spent in custody and the second half is spent in the community under the supervision of the YOT.

(6)   *National Framework*: section 41 established the Youth Justice Board. This board is the public body established to ensure the youth justice system is implemented and monitored, to promote good practice and to advise the Home Secretary on the setting of national standards.

Bainham identified three ways in which the Crime and Disorder Act 1998 reformed the youth justice system (Bainham, 2005: 630): (1) it made institutional changes to the criminal justice system by creating a Youth Justice Board and local youth offending teams; (2) it introduced measures for the prevention of crime and disorder in the form of child safety orders and child curfews; and (3) it reformed the options for dealing with young offenders by replacing cautioning with reprimands and final warnings. When a young person fails to respond to a final warning and reoffends, this will usually result in a prosecution in the youth court. The Crime and Disorder Act 1998 reflects the Labour Party's pre-1997 election promise to be 'tough on crime, tough on the causes of crime'. These conflicting and varied purposes result in a youth justice system that is ambiguous in terms of what it is trying to achieve. On the one hand it has created a youth justice system which is increasingly characterised by a culture of control and an atmosphere of hostility towards children and young people. Interventions which are supposed to be directed towards preventing youth crime rely on punitive and custodial measures. For example, the abolition of *doli incapax* (discussed in Chapter 5), coupled with the low age of criminal responsibility, places England and Wales further out of step with most jurisdictions in the rest of Europe. The 1998 Act contains a range of orders such as the anti-social behaviour order, the child safety order and the child curfew, where there is no requirement for the commission of, or conviction for, a criminal offence. However the 1998 Act also provides the basis for earlier intervention in the lives of young people and their parents aimed at alleviating the causes of crime. The development of YOTs in every local authority area has allowed for the provision of youth crime prevention initiatives which aim to strengthen schools, support parents, combat alcohol and drug abuse, create employment and training opportunities for young people and provide leisure activities. The 1998 Act also provides a voice for victims of youth offending, allowing victims to have the opportunity to confront the offender with the impact of their behaviour thus giving the youth justice system a restorative tone.

   The main youth justice provisions of the Crime and Disorder Act 1998 and subsequent Acts will be discussed throughout the rest of this book. Given the variety and extent of the reforms, some aspects of the youth justice system will be discussed in more detail than others, although this does not necessarily suggest any particular weighting of importance.

*Table 3.1*   Important dates in the development of the youth justice system, 1967 to present

| | |
|---|---|
| 1967 | In the United States of America, the *President's Commission on Law Enforcement and Administration of Justice: Task Force Report* stated that 'the juvenile court is a court of law'.<br>In *re Gault* (387 US 1 (1967)) the US Supreme Court ruled that where a juvenile faced incarceration, the juvenile should be entitled to the protection of due process of law, in the same way as adults. |
| 1982 | The Criminal Justice Act 1982 recognised that the juvenile court should be adversarial, children should have legal representation in court, imposed restrictions on social worker's discretion and ensured that any sentence was proportionate to the offence. The 1982 Act abolished borstals replacing them with youth custody centres. |
| 1988 | The Criminal Justice Act 1988 made it more difficult to impose custodial sentences on young offenders and introduced young offenders institutions which replaced youth custody centres. |
| 1989 | The Children Act 1989 removed from the juvenile court the power to order a young person into the care of a local authority. |
| 1991 | The Criminal Justice Act 1991 created a new youth court and extended its jurisdiction to young people under 18 years of age. |
| 1993 | The Criminal Justice Act 1993 reinstated the power of the court to take account of offenders' previous criminal records. |
| 1994 | The Criminal Justice and Public Order Act 1994 lowered the age at which children could be detained in custody for grave crimes such as manslaughter or other crimes of violence from 14 to 10 years of age and introduced a range of new measures which extended the courts' remand and sentencing powers to younger offenders. |
| 1998 | The Crime and Disorder Act 1998 introduced youth offending teams, the Youth Justice Board, parenting orders, child safety orders, local child curfew schemes and detention and training orders. It abolished the presumption of *doli incapax* and allowed courts to draw inferences from the failure of an accused child to give evidence or answer questions at trial. |
| 1999 | The Youth Justice and Criminal Evidence Act 1999 introduced the referral order as a new primary sentencing disposal for 10–17 year olds pleading guilty and convicted for the first time. |
| 2000 | The Powers of Criminal Courts (Sentencing) Act 2000 provides that the referral order is to become the standard sentence for all first time offenders under the age of 18 years unless their offending is so serious that it warrants custody. |
| 2001 | The Criminal Justice and Police Act 2001 raised the age limit of child curfew schemes to cover unsupervised children up to and including the age of 15. |
| 2008 | The Criminal Justice and Immigration Act 2008 introduced the youth rehabilitation order (YRO) as the new generic community sentence for young offenders. |

**Discussion topic**

Compare and contrast the approach to youth offending adopted by the Children and Young Persons Act 1969 and the Crime and Disorder Act 1998.

*Comment*

The Children and Young Persons Act 1969 aimed to decriminalise youth offending and encouraged maximum intervention by social workers in the lives of young people. The Crime and Disorder Act 1998 encourages earlier intervention in the lives of young people and their families. The 1998 Act introduced a number of orders to control anti-social, as opposed to criminal behaviour. The 1998 Act places an increased emphasis on responsibility for offending including both the young person and their family. For example, the 1998 Act abolished the concept of *doli incapax* and replaced cautions with a system of reprimands and final warnings. This contrasts with the approach of the 1969 Act which aimed to provide young people with the support and services which they previously had been denied.

**Suggested further reading**

Bedingfield, D. (1998) *The Child in Need, Children, The State and the Law* Bristol: Family Law, pp. 472–80.

Morgan, R. and Newburn, T. (2007) 'Youth Justice' in Maguire, M., Morgan, R. and Reiner, R. (eds) *The Oxford Handbook of Criminology* Oxford: Oxford University Press, pp. 1024–60.

Muncie, J. (2002) 'Children's rights and youth justice' in Franklin, B. (ed.) *The New Handbook of Children's Rights: Comparative Policy and Practice* London: Routledge, pp. 81–96.

# Part II
# Legal principles underpinning the English youth justice system

# 4 The impact of international law on the development of the English youth justice system

## Introduction

Various instruments of international law provide guidance on how countries should respond to youth offending. These include instruments which are binding on states and those that represent non-binding statements of practice. These instruments of international law relate to all aspects of the youth justice system from early intervention, diversion, restorative justice, right to a fair trial and conditions in detention. Chapter 4 will provide an introduction to the principles of international law which relate to the youth justice system. These principles will be discussed in more detail in each of the relevant chapters throughout the rest of the book.

## Historical development of international law on children's rights

The First World War (1914–18) was, at the time, the largest and bloodiest war the world had seen, and afterwards, there was a determination to set up international bodies to arbitrate disputes between nations and to prevent wars through negotiation. The League of Nations was set up in 1920 with a mandate to reduce armaments, to preserve all members against aggression and to impose economic and diplomatic sanctions against any member who broke these conditions. In 1919 a Committee for the Protection of Children was set up by the League of Nations. This was followed in 1924 by the League of Nations 'Declaration of the Rights of the Child'. The intention of the Declaration was not to create a binding treaty but to create guiding principles (Buck, 2005: 12). Article 1 of the 1924 Declaration requires that the child must be given the means requisite for its normal development, both materially and spiritually. Article 2 requires that the 'delinquent child must be reclaimed'. The Declaration directs states to create the conditions necessary for children to develop into citizens who will contribute to the community.

At the end of Second World War (1939–45), especially after the exposure of the horrors of the Nazi concentration camps and the Holocaust, there was a new commitment to form an international community, which would encompass all states of the world and which would have real power to prevent new wars by settling disputes through international mediation and arbitration, rather than through war. There was also a new commitment to ideas of human rights and the notion of equality among people. On 10 December 1948, the General Assembly of the United Nations voted 48 to 0 to adopt the Universal Declaration of Human Rights. The 1948 United Nations Declaration of Human Rights codified human rights for the first time on an international level, stating that everyone had rights due to them, not because of the property they owned, the colour of their skin or their sex but simply because they were human. Being human gives people certain inalienable rights, such as the right to life or the right to freedom of conscience. It was also believed that these rights needed to be written down and given legal status in order to prevent any of the atrocities of the Second World War happening again. The 1924 Declaration on the Rights of the Child was revised by the United Nations in 1959 in the form of a new Declaration of the Rights of the Child, which states in its preamble that 'mankind owes to the child the best it has to give' and that childhood is entitled to special care and assistance. Principle two requires that the best interest of the child shall be a paramount consideration.

## United Nations Convention on the Rights of the Child

Drafting of the United Nations Convention on the Rights of the Child began in 1978 and was completed in 1989 and has been ratified by 193 states, with the exception of Somalia and the United States of America. The UN Convention represents the most comprehensive legally binding statement of children's rights. The UN Convention states that all children have the same rights as adults and, in addition, distinct rights that apply to all human beings under the age of 18 years. The Convention recognises that young people under this age may need special protection because of their age or emotional development. It aims to protect and promote children's rights and welfare through a set of principles made up of 54 legally binding articles. It covers children's health, education, nationality, and the role of the child in the family and society. The Convention has also led to the development of a wide range of new, supplementary international human rights agreements concerning children. These include special provision for especially vulnerable children such as child workers, child prostitutes, child soldiers, child refugees and young people who offend.

The Convention was ratified by the UK in 1991 and under international law this places an obligation on the government to comply with its principles and standards. However, as the Convention has not been incorporated into domestic law, it is not legally enforceable in UK courts. Instead the UK government must periodically report to the United Nations Committee on the Rights of the Child on its progress in fulfilling its obligations under the Convention.

The preamble of the UN Convention recalls that the Universal Declaration of Human Rights 1948 proclaims: 'Childhood is entitled to special care and assistance'. In accordance with this ideal, the UN Convention emphasises the need for a child-centred youth justice system, as distinct from a punitive system, in which the child's interests are paramount and the inherent dignity of the child is preserved. The Convention prohibits the use of the death penalty and life imprisonment for young people and requires that any period of imprisonment be for the shortest appropriate period of time and only be imposed as a measure of last resort. Where detention is used, children must be protected from harm and must be treated with humanity and respect. The rest of this chapter will examine the main provisions of international law which are relevant to the operation of the youth justice system in England and Wales.

## Protect the best interests of the child

Article 3 of the United Nations Convention states that 'in all actions concerning children whether undertaken by public or private social welfare institutions, courts of law, administrative bodies or legislative bodies, the best interests of the child shall be the paramount consideration.' According to the UN Committee on the Rights of the Child, Article 3 requires that the traditional objectives of criminal justice must give way to rehabilitation and restorative justice objectives in dealing with young offenders (United Nations Committee on the Rights of the Child, 2007). Furthermore Article 40 of the Convention on the Rights of the Child requires states to promote the 'dignity and worth' of any child alleged, accused or recognised as having committed a criminal offence. The principles and provisions of the UN Convention on the Rights of the Child are informed by a number of more detailed Standards and Guidelines, for example the United Nations Standard Minimum Rules for the Administration of Juvenile Justice (the Beijing Rules) 1985 and the United Nations Guidelines for the Prevention of Juvenile Delinquency (the Riyadh Guidelines) 1990. Although the Beijing Rules and the Riyadh Guidelines are purely recommendatory and are non-binding in that they have no direct legal impact upon either international or national legislative bodies, they serve to identify current international thinking on human rights for young people and they represent the minimum recommended standards on youth justice issues. The Beijing Rules stress the well-being of the young person as paramount in decision-making as well as the importance of socio-education and extra-judicial approaches to youth crime. Article 52 of the Riyadh Guidelines requires governments to enact laws that promote the well-being of all young people. In 2008 the Council of Europe adopted the European Rules for Juvenile Offenders subject to Sanctions or Measures (Recommendation CM/Rec (2008) 11). The European Rules set out fundamental principles to be followed by states in their treatment of young people in conflict with the law, including a requirement that the imposition and implementation of sanctions or measures be based on the best interests of the young person. This issue of protecting the best interest of young people who have engaged in offending behaviour will be examined in more detail in Chapter 6.

## Support families and involve communities

Article 18.2 of the UN Convention sets out the obligations of the state to assist families in raising their children:

> States Parties shall render appropriate assistance to parents and legal guardians in the performance of their child-rearing responsibilities and shall ensure the development of institutions, facilities and services for the care of children.

This provision is complemented by Article 1.2 of the Beijing Rules 1985 which stresses the idea that the state should ensure a productive life for young people within the community, such as to encourage in them a process of personal development and education 'during that period in life when she or he is most susceptible to deviant behaviour'. The Beijing rules point to the important role that a constructive social policy for young people could play in tackling youth offending. The Riyadh Guidelines also support preventive policies which facilitate the successful socialisation and integration of all young people, in particular through the family. Article 33 states that 'Communities should provide . . . a wide range of community-based support measures for young persons, including community development centres, recreational facilities and services designed in view of the special problems of children in a situation of social risk.' The child's right to special protection is reiterated in other non-child specific human rights documents, such as the United Nations Standard Minimum Rules for Non-custodial Measures (the Tokyo Rules) which promote greater community involvement in the management of the criminal justice system, specifically in the treatment of offenders, as well as promoting a sense of responsibility among offenders towards society. The Tokyo Rules emphasise the principle of minimum intervention. The United Nations Declaration of Basic Principles of Justice for Victims of Crime and Abuse of Power 1985 is also relevant as it considers one of its principal aims to be the promotion of community efforts and public participation in crime prevention.

These broad fundamental perspectives refer to comprehensive social policy in general and aim at promoting the young person's welfare to the greatest possible extent, which will minimise the necessity of intervention by the youth justice system and, in turn, will reduce the harm that may be caused by any intervention. Such care measures for the young, before the onset of youth offending behaviour, are basic policy requisites designed to avoid the need for the application of these instruments of international law.

## Age-appropriate treatment

Article 40(3) provides that young offenders must be treated in a manner consistent with the promotion of the 'child's sense of dignity and worth . . . and which takes into account the child's age'. Article 40 thus requires age-appropriate treatment of children in conflict with the law. Article 40(3) also requires states to establish an age of criminal responsibility below which children will be presumed not to have the capacity to infringe the criminal law. This is an issue which will be explored in more detail in Chapter 5. Article 40 of the Convention on the Rights of the Child recognises the traditional right to due process and provides that children have the right to have charges explained to them. Under Article 40 the principles of a fair and just trial apply explicitly to proceedings involving children. The United Nations Committee on the Rights of the Child (2007: 23) clearly requires that due process for children involves that those working in the trial process, including the police, judiciary, lawyers, social workers and probation officers, receive regular training. It also requires that decisions are made without delay and with the involvement of the parents. Privacy must be respected throughout all stages of the proceedings.

The International Covenant on Civil and Political Rights was adopted by the United Nations in 1966. It makes reference to the need for young people to receive treatment appropriate to their age and legal status. Article 10(3) requires that young offenders should be segregated from adults and accorded treatment appropriate to their age and legal status. Article 10(2)(b) also requires that young people accused of a crime should be separated from adults and brought to justice as speedily as possible.

## Diversion

Article 40(3) of the Convention on the Rights of the Child requires state parties to develop measures for dealing with young people who offend without resorting to judicial proceedings. A variety of dispositions such as care, guidance, supervision orders, counselling, probation, foster care, educational and vocational training programmes and other alternatives to institutional care should be available to ensure that children are dealt with in a manner appropriate to their well-being and proportionate to both their circumstances and the offence. The UN Committee on the Rights of the Child has recommended that diversion from the criminal justice system should be a core objective of every youth justice system and this should be explicitly stated in legislation (United Nations Committee on the Rights of the Child, 2007: 24).

Article 37 of the Convention on the Rights of the Child requires that detention must be used only as a measure of last resort. Again this issue will be examined in detail in Chapter 10. The Convention details a variety of dispositions which ought to be used instead of custody, including care, probation, guidance, foster care, educational and vocational training. The UN Rules for the Protection of Juveniles Deprived of their Liberty (the Havana Rules) 1990 require that detention should only be used in exceptional cases where the child is accused of committing a serious act of violence against another person or of persistence in committing other serious offences and unless there is no other appropriate response. The Havana Rules emphasise the importance of the independence of prosecutors in promoting diversion from criminal proceedings for young people up to 18 years of age. Rule 17(1)(c) of the Beijing Rules states that the deprivation of liberty directly conflicts with the aims of the Convention and that accordingly a custodial sentence should only be imposed as a sanction for serious acts of violence. In 2006 the UN Secretary-General's study on Violence Against Children highlighted the high level of physical violence and punishment experienced by children in custody and recommended that efforts be made to prevent this violence (United Nations Secretary General, 2006).

The United Nations Guidelines for the Prevention of Juvenile Delinquency (the Riyadh Guidelines) 1990 emphasise that policies should avoid criminalising and penalising a child for behaviour that does not cause serious damage to the development of the child or to others. The Riyadh Guidelines stress that the successful prevention of juvenile delinquency requires efforts on the part of the entire society to ensure the harmonious development of adolescents with respect for, and promotion of, their personality from early childhood. By engaging in lawful, socially useful activities and adopting a humanistic orientation towards society, young people can develop non-criminogenic attitudes. The Riyadh Guidelines recommend that policies and measures should involve the provision of opportunities to meet the varying needs of young people and to serve as a supportive framework for safeguarding the personal development of all young people, particularly those who are demonstrably endangered or at social risk and are in need of special care and protection.

## Child's voice must be heard

Article 12 of the UN Convention requires that the child's voice is heard and taken into account in all decision-making. Article 12.1 of the Convention requires the involvement of the child in any decision-making: 'any child who is capable of forming his or her own views' has the right to express those views freely and for their views to be given due weight in accordance with the age and maturity of the child.

The UN Convention and other international instruments are clearly based on a 'welfare' approach underpinned by three core principles: recognition that children's status is different from adults, emphasis on children's welfare and participation of children in all decisions affecting them. The philosophy that directs the general principles of the United Nations

Convention, Rules, Guidelines, Declarations and Resolutions is essentially based on the protection of the personality of all young people below 18 years of age and on the mobilisation of existing resources within the community. These instruments of international law emphasise the need for youth crime policies and interventions to avoid a narrow focus on the crime and to take into account the social and contextual factors that are frequently associated with youth offending. All of these United Nations Conventions, Rules, Guidelines, Declarations and Resolutions on youth justice and responses to children who offend consistently stress the principle of decriminalisation and diversion. Thus under international law states should only imprison young people as a measure of last resort. International law requires the UK to have a system for diverting young people from imprisonment and the youth courts and promote the fulfilment of each young person's potential.

However these instruments of international law are too vague on detention as a last resort, too weak on the age of criminal responsibility and are incomplete on the trial process, sentencing and serious crimes committed by children. This weakness has allowed youth justice law and policy in England and Wales to focus primarily on retaliatory responses to youth crime. Young offenders have been conceptualised as violent predators warranting retribution, rather than as wayward children in need of a guiding hand (Arthur, 2004). This attitude towards young offenders has ensured that policy and practice in relation to children in trouble is concentrated upon punishment, retribution and the wholesale incarceration of children, contrary to the provisions and principles of the UN Convention. The UN Committee has expressed concern that in England and Wales the age at which children enter the criminal justice system is low, that an increasing number of children are being detained in custody at earlier ages for lesser offences and for longer sentences, that children between 12 and 14 years of age are being deprived of their liberty, and that deprivation of liberty is not being used only as a measure of last resort and for the shortest appropriate period of time (United Nations Committee on the Rights of the Child, 2002: 59). England and Wales has not only one of the lowest ages of criminal responsibility, but also locks up more young people than most other countries in Western Europe. The institutions of incarceration – young offenders institutions – are characterised by appalling conditions, over-crowding, brutality, suicide and self-harm. In summary the youth justice system in England and Wales has developed into a formal and rigid system which draws younger children into contact with the youth justice system and escalates them up the sentencing ladder and into custody.

The United Nations Convention on the Rights of the Child and the associated Rules and Guidelines are not a part of UK national law, therefore it is not possible to bring a challenge in the UK courts where there are grounds for believing that the state is violating Convention rights. The Convention is persuasive, but breach attracts no formal sanction. The UN Convention may be the most ratified of international human rights covenants, however it is also the most violated (Muncie, 2007: 30). This is not to say that the rights in the Convention are totally without protection. The Convention is still a legally binding treaty, and not merely a declaration. State parties have

*Table 4.1* Provisions of international law relevant to the English youth justice system

| | |
|---|---|
| United Nations Convention on the Rights of the Child | Preamble: 'Childhood is entitled to special care and assistance'. <br> Article 3: 'in all actions concerning children whether undertaken by public or private social welfare institutions, courts of law, administrative bodies or legislative bodies, the best interests of the child shall be the paramount consideration'. <br> Article 18.2: 'States Parties shall render appropriate assistance to parents and legal guardians in the performance of their child-rearing responsibilities and shall ensure the development of institutions, facilities and services for the care of children.' <br> Article 37: imprisonment shall be used 'as a measure of last resort'. <br> Article 40 requires states to promote the 'dignity and worth' of any child alleged, accused or recognised as having committed a criminal offence. |
| United Nations Standard Minimum Rules for the Administration of Juvenile Justice (the Beijing Rules) 1985 | Article 1.2 stresses the idea that the state should ensure a productive life for young people within the community such as to encourage in them a process of personal development and education 'during that period in life when she or he is most susceptible to deviant behaviour'. <br> Article 4.1 requires that the age of criminal responsibility not to be set at too low an age level. <br> Article 17.1a: any action taken against young offenders should be proportionate, not only to the 'circumstances and gravity' of the offence, but to the 'circumstances and the needs of the juvenile'. |
| United Nations Guidelines for the Prevention of Juvenile Delinquency (the Riyadh Guidelines) 1990 | Article 33: 'Communities should provide … a wide range of community-based support measures for young persons, including community development centres, recreational facilities and services designed in view of the special problems of children in a situation of social risk.' |
| United Nations Standard Minimum Rules for Non-custodial Measures (the Tokyo Rules) 1990 | Emphasises the principle of minimum intervention. |
| United Nations Declaration of Basic Principles of Justice for Victims of Crime and Abuse of Power 1985 | Promotion of community efforts and public participation in crime prevention. |

a legal obligation to put these rights of the child into effect. The United Nations Committee on the Rights of the Child monitors how states are making progress in securing Convention rights for children within their jurisdiction. The principal function of the Committee is to assess the extent to which states are implementing the Convention, to report on this progress and to make recommendations for future improvements to how states implement the Convention. The United Nations Committee on the Rights of the Child has repeatedly recommended that the UK establish a system of juvenile justice that fully integrates into its legislation, policies and practice the provisions and principles of the Convention, the Beijing Rules and the Riyadh Guidelines (United Nations Committee on the Rights of the Child, 2002).

International law could potentially advance the rights of young people and create a just youth justice system that is more child-centred. Youth crime will only be prevented if we are prepared to take these young people's rights more seriously. As Cunneen and White asserted: 'if young people's rights are not respected . . . then why should they respect law and state institutions?' (Cunneen and White, 1995: 267). Proper implementation of the instruments of international law examined in this chapter could have important consequences for the delivery of youth justice, creating a system that is inclusive and diversionary. The youth justice system should be based on a human rights framework which would provide a clear set of principles upon which law, policy and practice could consistently be based. The aim must be to establish an effective children's rights centered system for treating children in trouble with the law that complies with Britain's international law obligations. Systems for responding to juveniles who are in trouble with the law that are purely punitive in intent, including the use of custody, are neither in the best interests of the child or society and are incompatible with children's human rights.

---

### Discussion topic

What are the main aims and standards expressed in international youth justice law?

---

### *Comment*

The international law examined in this chapter requires states to ensure that law, policy and practice in the area of youth justice protect the rights of all children, promote their development, ensure their best interests are a primary concern at all times, and that the child's views are taken into account in all decision-making affecting them. International law also stresses the need for procedural guarantees. For example, Article 40 of the

United Nations Convention on the Rights of the Child includes a detailed series of due process guarantees. States are required to establish specialist laws and institutions for young people in conflict with the law and the adoption of measures to divert such young people from the criminal justice system. International law also requires children's reintegration into society as a core aim of youth justice policy.

## Suggested further reading

Archard, D. (2007) 'Children's Rights and Juvenile Justice' in Hill, M., Lockyer, A. and Stone, F. *Youth Justice and Child Protection*, London: Jessica Kingsley.

Buck, T. (2005) *International Child Law*, London: Routledge, pp. 47–73.

Verhellen, E. (2006) *Convention on the Rights of the Child*, Antwerp: Garant, pp. 63–104.

# 5 The age of criminal responsibility and the defence of *doli incapax*

## Introduction

To be convicted of a criminal offence the defendant must have performed the *actus reus* and *mens rea* of the offence and have no defence available to them. All of these elements must be proved beyond all reasonable doubt. *Actus reus* is the guilty conduct of a defendant. *Mens rea* is the mental element required by the definition of the crime. *Mens rea* is the device through which those who are thought to be deserving of punishment, because of their responsibility and their moral blameworthiness, are identified. *Mens rea* has evolved into a requirement of positive culpability on the part of the defendant. In a general sense *mens rea* approximates closely to the broader idea of 'blame'. Just because someone may have committed the *actus reus* and *mens rea* of an offence does not necessarily mean that they are guilty of that offence, they may have a valid defence. One such defence is the defence of infancy, or *doli incapax*, which precludes infants from criminal liability for their actions. The minimum age of criminal responsibility is the minimum age at which the law allows criminal proceedings to be brought against a child who commits a crime. Children below the minimum age of criminal responsibility are considered to be *doli incapax*, that is 'incapable of committing an evil act'. Children below the minimum age of criminal responsibility cannot be held legally responsible for their behaviour, regardless of the behaviour of the children.

Chapter 5 will examine the age of criminal responsibility in England and Wales. This chapter will consider how the age of criminal responsibility in England compares with other countries. Chapter 5 will also examine the history of the defence of *doli incapax*.

## The age of criminal responsibility

You will recall from Chapter 1 that the pre-Norman Laws of Ine dating from the eight century suggest the age of 10 years as the age of criminal responsibility. This was the age at which young offenders could be held criminally responsible for their actions. The tenth-century Laws of Athelstan, drafted by a bishop, provided that a thief should not be spared punishment if he is over 12 years old. Bracton's thirteenth-century treatise does not specify a minimum age of criminal responsibility but does refer to children being protected from the criminal law by virtue of their 'harmlessness of intention' (Walker, 1999: 135–6). By the fifteenth century the pre-Norman age limits had been lowered to seven years of age. Other than this, the criminal law accorded no differentiations in the method of bringing offenders to trial, in the form of the trial itself and in the punishment that could be enforced. Young offenders were liable to the same forms of trial and punishments, including capital conviction, transportation and imprisonment. Once a child was aged seven years the child was held responsible for any misdemeanour or crimes they committed. If children were old enough to commit a crime, then they were considered old enough to be sentenced the same as adults.

Section 50 of the Children and Young Persons Act 1933 raised the age of criminal responsibility from seven to eight years. The Criminal Justice Act 1963 raised the age to 10 years old. The Children and Young Persons Act 1969 proposed raising the age to 14 years, but this part of the 1969 Act never became law. Currently, in England and Wales the minimum age of criminal responsibility is 10 years of age. However in England and Wales it is possible to regulate the behaviour of children under 10 years of age. Section 11 of the Crime and Disorder Act 1998 allows children under the age of 10 to be subject to child safety orders where they have either breached a curfew or committed what would have been a crime had they been ten or over and have acted in an anti-social manner. Acting anti-socially means acting in a way likely to cause alarm, distress or harassment. Such measures are justified on the basis that '[c]hildren under 10 need help to change their bad behaviour just as much as older children' (Home Office, 1997a: 99). Local child curfew schemes also allow for children under the age of 10 years to be controlled. The curfew schemes prohibit children under ten years of age from being in public after a specified hour unless accompanied by an adult. In this context the concept of the age of criminal responsibility has been eroded.

The age of criminal responsibility varies from country to country:

*Table 5.1* Age of criminal responsibility

| | |
|---|---|
| 7 years | Cyprus, India, Liechtenstein, Nigeria, Singapore, South Africa, Switzerland |
| 8 years | Scotland, Gibraltar, Kenya, Sri Lanka |
| 10 years | England and Wales, Australia, Fiji, Malaysia, New Zealand |
| 12 years | Canada, Greece, Republic of Ireland, Jamaica, Netherlands, Turkey |
| 14 years | Austria, China, Germany, Italy, Latvia, Lithuania, Romania, Vietnam |
| 15 years | Denmark, Egypt, Estonia, Finland, Iceland, Norway, Sweden |
| 16 years | Argentina, Poland, Portugal, Spain |
| 18 years | Belgium, Brazil, Colombia, Luxembourg, Peru |

## Doli incapax

It is clear from Table 5.1 that the minimum age of criminal responsibility in England and Wales is much lower than most other countries in Europe and many countries worldwide. However, comparing the ages of criminal responsibility of different countries only gives a partial view of the way the criminal justice system treats young offenders. The English youth justice system has traditionally not prosecuted young people once they have achieved the age of criminal responsibility. Instead the presumption of *doli incapax* was invoked. According to the legal doctrine of *doli incapax*, children did not become fully criminally responsible for their actions once they reached the age of criminal responsibility. They would only be held criminally responsible if in addition to committing the *actus reus* and *mens rea* of a criminal offence, the prosecution could also prove, beyond all reasonable doubt, that when doing the act, the child knew that what they were doing was seriously wrong. Thus at common law a child below the age of 7 was considered *doli incapax*, a child between 7 and 14 was presumed *doli incapax* as at this age children were considered incapable of identifying right from wrong, and therefore lacked the necessary criminal intent necessary for prosecution.

The presumption of *doli incapax* allows the prosecution the opportunity to prove, beyond any reasonable doubt, that at the time of the alleged offence the child was aware that what he or she was doing was seriously wrong as opposed to being merely mischievous or naughty. In an early criminal law textbook, Kenny's *Outlines of Criminal Law*, the author talks of the issue being of a child having a 'guilty mind' and equates this with 'mischievous discretion' the test of which is: 'Had he a guilty knowledge that he was doing wrong?' (Turner, 1958: 74). In *Blackstone* the test was described as whether the child was able to discern between good and evil based on the strength of the child's understanding and judgement (Blackstone, 1769: 23–4). The modern test upon which *doli incapax* was based was: did the child know that the act was wrong – not merely wrong but 'gravely wrong, seriously wrong' (*Gorrie* (1918) 83 JP 186). Glanville Williams argues that the rule in *Gorrie* refers to the child knowing that their behaviour was morally wrong, for although a child may be able to distinguish between slight and grave degrees of moral wrong, the child can hardly be expected to distinguish between slight and grave degrees of legal wrong. A child will know nothing of the classification of crimes and punishments. This suggests that the test of knowledge of 'grave wrong' is a moral test (Williams, 1954: 494). The presumption existed to protect children from suffering the full extent of the law in a time when the death penalty was equally applicable to children as it was to adults. The standard of proof required to rebut the presumption of *doli incapax* is the criminal standard of proving beyond a reasonable doubt. The nearer the child is to the age of 10 years the stronger the evidence required to rebut the presumption.

The Divisional Court held in *A v DPP* ([1997] Crim LR 125) that knowledge that an act was seriously wrong could not be presumed from the mere commission of the offence, notwithstanding how horrifying or obviously wrong the act was. However it could be inferred from the surrounding circumstances of the offence. This case involved a 12-year-old boy who, along with two other boys, subjected a 12-year-old girl to an indecent assault. The offence was committed against a background of threats, the victim's obvious distress and the victim was taken some distance away to a remote place where intervention by others was unlikely. These surrounding circumstances were sufficient for the court to conclude that the defendant knew what he was doing was seriously wrong and that the presumption of *doli incapax* had been rebutted. The presumption of *doli incapax* could also be rebutted by proof that a child was of normal mental capacity for their age. In *JM (A Minor) v Runeckles* ((1984) 79 Cr App R 255) a 13-year-old girl hit the victim with a milk bottle and ran away from the police. She was later apprehended by the police and gave a statement which accurately reflected the victim's account of the incident. The Divisional Court found that this was sufficient evidence to rebut the presumption that a child under 14 years of age was incapable of forming criminal intent. However, merely running away would not be sufficient evidence to rebut the presumption (*A v Sharples* [1992] Crim LR 34). In *L (A Minor) v DPP* ([1997] Crim LR 127) the Divisional Court held that it was for the court to decide whether what the child did or said before or after the commission of the offence indicated his state of mind at the time of the offence and his appreciation of the seriousness of his actions. Guilty knowledge that an act was wrong could be determined from a police interview, thus there was no need for the evidence of a teacher or psychiatrist. Any admission by the child to the police regarding knowledge that the crime is wrong would be admissible. The child's home environment may also be used to prove whether or not the child knew right from wrong; if the child were brought up in a 'good home' the presumption is more likely to be rebutted (*F v Padwick* [1959] Crim LR 439; *B v R* (1958) 44 Cr App R 1).

Towards the end of the twentieth century the effectiveness and appropriateness of *doli incapax* was being questioned. In the case of *C (A Minor) v DPP* ([1994] 3 All ER 190), which concerned the actions of a 12-year-old boy who had been caught with a companion tampering with a motorbike, Mr Justice Laws in the High Court ruled that the presumption of *doli incapax* was 'no longer part of the law of England'. Laws J believed that arguing a child of 14 years of age would not appreciate the moral obliquity of his actions was out of touch with today's society and contrary to common sense. Laws J argued that:

> whatever may have been the position in an earlier age, when there was no system of universal compulsory education and when perhaps children

did not grow up as quickly as they do nowadays, this presumption at the present time is a serious disservice to our law.

([1994] 3 All ER 190, 196)

Laws J continued to describe the presumption as 'unreal and contrary to common sense', looked upon by 'modern judges . . . with increasing unease and perhaps rank disapproval', 'in principle objectionable', 'out of step with the general law', 'conceptually obscure', 'full of disturbing, even nonsensical implications', 'representative of a bizarre state of affairs', indicative of a state of law 'we should be ashamed of', capable of giving 'rise to the risk of injustice', 'divisive and perverse', an 'outdated and unprincipled presumption', and with no 'utility whatever in the present era'.

However the House of Lords in *C (A Minor) v DPP* did not share the view that the presumption was detrimental to the English legal system and overturned Justice Laws decision in an appeal and reinstated the presumption stating that '*doli incapax* was a rule of the common law that could only be abrogated by statute' ([1995] 1 AC 1). The case was decided on the grounds of legal propriety and the respective roles of the judiciary and parliament, rather than because of any merits that the presumption bestowed. Indeed Lord Lowry in the House of Lords states 'the presumption has in recent years been the object of some logical and forceful criticisms' and that 'the courts . . . often treat the rebuttal as a formality'. He stated further that the presumption 'is not, and never has been, completely logical' and he argued that the 'time has come to examine further a doctrine which appears to have been inconsistently applied and which is certainly capable of producing inconsistent results' ([1995] 1 AC 1, 33, 39). He concluded with the hope that 'my survey may help to provide the incentive for a much-needed new look at an undoubted problem' ([1995] 1 AC 1, 40). Similarly in the House of Lords, Lord Jauncey described the rule as 'an affront to common sense'. Nonetheless the House of Lords ruled that abolishing the presumption of *doli incapax* was a significant change to the law and thus was a matter for parliament to consider rather than the judiciary.

In the White Paper *No More Excuses* the Labour Party made several recommendations about improving the youth justice system (Home Office, 1997a). One aspect of this radical reorganisation was to modernise 'the archaic rule of *doli incapax*'; the government believed that the 'notion of *doli incapax* is contrary to common sense' which is 'not in the interests of justice, or victims or of young people themselves' (Home Office, 1997a: 4.4). Following this White Paper came the Crime and Disorder Act 1998, section 34 of which abolished the presumption of *doli incapax*. Section 34 thus means that a child aged 10 years of age can be considered as legally responsible for their actions as an adult. Such a child is no longer presumed incapable of evil. Thus we have a law 'which holds that a person is completely irresponsible on the day before his tenth birthday, and fully responsible as soon as the jelly and ice-cream have been cleared away the following day' (Smith, 1994: 427). The abolition of *doli incapax* removes an important principle which had acted to protect children from the full rigour of the criminal law. Bandalli argues that the abolition of *doli incapax* reflects a steady erosion of the special consideration afforded to children, extends the remit of the criminal law to address all manner of problems which young people face and is 'symbolic of the state's limited vision in understanding children, the nature of childhood or the true meaning of an appropriate criminal law response' (Bandalli, 2000: 94). Bandalli stressed that the presumption of *doli incapax* operated in a protective manner 'shielding the child from the damage that might otherwise be done by being absorbed into the criminal justice system'. Its removal makes 'childhood irrelevant to criminalisation'. She argues that the trend towards using the criminal law to address social problems should not be extended to the treatment of young people, as it inevitably shifts responsibility onto the shoulders of the child, thus denying 'the responsibility of the rest of us' (Bandalli, 1998).

### *The defence of* doli incapax

In the case of *DPP v P* ([2007] EWHC 946) the court questioned whether or not the defence of *doli incapax* still exists in law. Smith LJ took the view in this case that although Parliament has abolished the presumption of *doli incapax*, the defence of *doli incapax* still remains. Any comments made by Smith LJ were, by her own admission, *obiter dicta* as the 'court had not had the benefit of full argument on the issue', but she concluded that although the Crime and Disorder Act 1998 had abolished the presumption of *doli incapax*, it had not abolished the defence which remains available. Smith LJ's argument is based on a literal interpretation of section 34. Smith observes that the subject in section 34 is 'the rebuttable presumption of criminal law' and the verb 'is abolished' can only apply to the subject. Accordingly it is the presumption that has been abolished. Thus, according to Smith LJ young people can raise a defence of *doli incapax*, with the burden of proof resting on the young person to prove that they were *doli incapax*. However, as stated above, these comments were merely *obiter*. Also, in 1997 the government in the White Paper *No More Excuses* made explicit their desire to abolish the presumption rather than reversing it. The government explicitly rejected the reverse burden scheme, thus Smith LJ's interpretation of section 34 could not possibly have been intended by the government. Consideration was given by the government to retaining the defence but the government made clear in 1997 that it preferred outright abolition because this was the 'simplest course and would send a clear signal that in general children of 10 and over should be held accountable for their own actions' (Home Office, 1997a: 15). The government was also concerned that retaining the defence would result in it being used often and therefore perpetuate difficulties prosecuting children under 14 years (Home Office, 1997b: 18).

The Court of Appeal specifically addressed this issue in *R v T* ([2008] EWCA Crim 815) in which case Latham LJ was emphatic that the defence of *doli incapax* had been abolished. Latham LJ concluded that:

> It is difficult to see ... how the abolition of the presumption was intended to result in anything other than the abolition of the concept of *doli incapax* as having any effect in law. In our view that accords with the way in which the matter was approached by Lord Lowry with unanimous approval of their Lordships in *C (A minor) v DPP*. In our judgment, accordingly, Parliament must be taken to have intended 'the presumption' to encompass the concept of *doli incapax* when it was abolished in Section 34.
>
> (at paragraph 20)

This Court of Appeal ruling was upheld by the House of Lords in *R v JTB* ([2009] UKHL 20) in which the House of Lords held that the presumption of *doli incapax* and the defence of *doli incapax* were two separate things. The House of Lords pointed out that section 34 of the Crime and Disorder Act 1998 was enacted in response to growing concerns about the extent to which the presumption of *doli incapax* placed an unfair burden on the prosecution. Accordingly, their Lordships concluded that the Crime and Disorder Act 1998 abolished both the presumption and the defence of *doli incapax*.

### Problems with the current law on doli incapax

England and Wales takes a markedly more punitive approach to this issue than comparable countries. The impact of the decisions in *DPP v P* and *R v T* is that young defendants with impaired mental capacity are exposed to the full rigours of the criminal justice system. This is exactly the type of situation in which the presumption could have acted as a safeguard. The abolition of *doli incapax* is based on the presumption that children are more worldly today and thus do not require the protection of *doli incapax* as they grow up quicker. Yet on the other hand children are more cosseted and protected and lack the freedom that characterised other generations. Children are receiving conflicting messages from media, computer games, TV etc. Can it be argued that children are more streetwise and mature than in the days of the Artful Dodger?

Do children qualify as moral agents? Can a child foresee the consequences of their actions – if not then can they make a moral evaluation? Until a young person is 16 years old they cannot consent to sexual relations or join the armed forces. The age at which you can buy cigarettes or alcohol or vote is 18 years. Children involved in crime, particularly persistent offenders, often experience difficult deprived backgrounds – including families who are fractured, traumatised and unable to cope with their challenging behaviour; physical and sexual abuse; periods in and out of care; behaviour and learning disorders; educational disengagement; truancy and exclusion from school. The legal scholar Professor Peter Arenella asks: 'Why should someone qualify as a moral agent if he lacks the capacity to deliberate about whether he should have acted differently?' (Arenella, 1990). Children under 14 years are not adults. Individuals vary but they are still developing in terms of cognitive capacity and emotional development and are much more impulsive. The more a young person is involved with crime, the greater the gap with adults tends to be. Yet when barely into their teens they can be put through and expected to understand a system geared to convicting and punishing adults. Moore argues that criminal liability should be avoided for a wrongful action if 'at the moment of such action's performance, one did not have sufficient capacity or opportunity to make the choice to do otherwise' (Moore, 1990). Moore viewed infancy as within the category of 'status excuses' concerning 'individuals who do not and cannot function well enough for us to confidently liken their actions and intentions to the actions and intention of sober, sane adults'.

Article 40 of the United Nations Convention on the Right of the Child requires each state to set a reasonable minimum age of criminal responsibility. The United Nations Standard Minimum Rules for the Administration of Juvenile Justice (the Beijing Rules) 1985 recommend that the minimum age of criminal responsibility shall not be fixed at too low an age level, bearing in mind the facts of emotional, mental and intellectual maturity. The important consideration, as outlined in Rule 17 of the Beijing Rules, is whether a child, by virtue of his or her individual discernment and understanding, can be held responsible for their behaviour. In line with this rule the UN Committee on the Rights of the Child has recommended state parties to increase their age of criminal responsibility to the age of 12 years as the absolute minimum age. The UN Committee also strongly recommended that states parties set a minimum age of criminal responsibility that does not allow, by way of exception, the use of a lower age (United Nations Committee on the Rights of the Child, 2007: 32–4). In its report in 2002 the UN Committee expressed that it was 'particularly concerned' about 'the abolition of the principle of *doli incapax*' and recommended that the age of criminal responsibility should be raised considerably (United Nations Committee on the Rights of the Child, 2002). However the European Court of Human Rights looked at the matter in *V and T v UK* ((2000) 3 EHRR 121) and recognised the variation in minimum ages across Europe and, though stating that the age of 10 years is at the lower end of the spectrum, held that 'it cannot be said to be so young as to differ disproportionately from the age limit followed in other European States' (at [74]).

Howard argues that 'no civilised society regards children as accountable for their actions to the same extent as adults' (Howard, 1982: 343). To apply the same standards to a 13 year old as an adult is to ignore large amounts of evidence about the immaturity of children at that age. Similarly Bandalli asserts that 'children are perceived as needing and receiving protection from the consequences of their immaturity in other areas of the law and this is equally appropriate for criminal responsibility' (Bandalli, 1998: 121). Terms such as 'intention' cannot and should not be applied without taking account of the large differences in capacity and judgment between adults and children. *Doli incapax* reflected a concern that 'using criminal penalties to punish a child who does not appreciate the wrongfulness of his or her actions lacks moral justification' (Penal Affairs Consortium, 1995: 5). The English youth justice system should urgently seek to learn from European neighbours that have higher ages of criminal responsibility and lower rates of offending. Since 1997 there has been a steady climb in the proportion of young offenders prosecuted rather than diverted from prosecution.

---

**Discussion topic**

The effect of section 34 of the Crime and Disorder Act 1998 was to abolish the presumption that a child was *doli incapax*, but not the defence itself.

---

*Comment*

Until 1998 all children in England and Wales aged 10 years but not yet 14 years were presumed to be *doli incapax*. This meant that to prosecute a child within this age group the prosecution had to rebut the presumption that a child was incapable of crime by proving beyond any reasonable doubt that the child understood their act was seriously wrong. Section 34 of the Crime and Disorder Act 1998 states that 'the rebuttable presumption of criminal law that a child aged 10 or over is incapable of committing an offence is hereby abolished'. In *R v T* ([2008] EWCA Crim 815) Latham LJ held that section 34 of the Crime and Disorder Act abolished the presumption and the defence of *doli incapax*.

**Suggested further reading**

Bandalli, S. (1998) 'Abolition of the presumption of *doli incapax* and the criminalisation of children', *Howard Journal of Criminal Justice*, 37, 2, 114–23.

Stokes, E. (2000) 'Abolishing the presumption of *doli incapax*: reflections on the death of a doctrine' in Pickford, J. (ed.) *Youth Justice: Theory and Practice*, London: Cavendish, pp. 51–74.

Telford, M. (2007) 'Youth justice: new shoots on a bleak landscape – Director of Public Prosecutions v P' *Child and Family Law Quarterly*, 19, 4, 505–17.

# 6   Protecting the welfare of young people who offend

## Introduction

Protecting the welfare of the child has traditionally been at the heart of youth justice systems. This chapter will consider the concept of the welfare of the child in terms of how young people are treated in youth offending cases. This chapter will also consider the importance of welfare concerns in the current youth justice system.

## The importance of protecting the welfare of young offenders

You will recall from Chapter 1 that, historically, young offenders were treated the same as adults: punishment was focused on deterrence rather than reform and children were convicted and punished as adults in adult courts. In the latter part of the nineteenth century it was acknowledged that children were uniquely vulnerable. Consequently child-centred and welfare-based treatments were developed. Welfare-based treatments require that all interventions should be directed to meeting the needs of young people, rather than responding solely to their deeds (Muncie, 2004: 257). Since the late nineteenth century the principles of acting in a child's best interests and making welfare considerations a paramount concern in court proceedings have underpinned the development of youth justice systems throughout the world. For example, as you studied in Chapter 1, in the United States of America the founders of the juvenile court assumed the role of benevolent parent and social worker rolled into one. The first official juvenile court judge asked 'why is it not the duty of the state, instead of asking merely whether a boy or a girl has committed a specific offence, to find out what he is physically, mentally, morally . . . ' (Mack, 1909). Using broad discretion, the early juvenile court judge was to provide the necessary help and guidance to a young person who might otherwise proceed further down the path of chronic crime (Fox, 1996). This view of young offenders was also prevalent in Canada in the early twentieth century. Section 38 of the Canadian Juvenile Delinquents Act 1908 states that 'every juvenile delinquent shall be treated not as a criminal, but as a misdirected and misguided child and one needing aid, encouragement, help and assistance ... ' During the Parliamentary debates surrounding the Canadian Act, protection of the child and the interests of society were presented as a means of achieving each other, it was believed that no distinction should be drawn between neglected and delinquent children, that all should be recognized as of the same class and should be dealt with in a manner which serves the best interests of the child (Scott, 1907–08).

Similarly in England, throughout most of the twentieth century young offenders were perceived as in need of protection and redirection rather than punishment. Section 44 of the Children and Young Persons Act 1933 imposes an important welfare principle which requires every court to have regard to the welfare of a child or young person who is brought before it, either as an offender or otherwise. The welfare principle's main virtue is that it requires a decision made with respect to a child to be justified from the point of view of a judgment about the child's interests. It would be inconsistent with the welfare principle to make a decision that is overtly justified by reference to the way the outcome benefited some other interests (Eekelaar, 2002). In England, the Children and Young Persons Act 1969 was also underpinned by a philosophy of treatment which removed any lingering distinction between children who offended and those who needed care and protection. The causes of offending and deprivation were seen as the same: both types of children suffered from essentially the same problems and had the same treatment needs. Section 1(2) of the 1969 Act provided that a civil care order or a supervision order could be made where the young person was guilty of an offence, excluding homicide. It also had to be proved that there was a need for care and control which the young offender was unlikely to receive unless a court order were made. The separate power to commit a child to care in criminal proceedings (section 7(7) Children and Young Persons Act 1969) also reflected a fundamental purpose in the legislation, which was to treat all children in trouble as children in need of care and protection. The influential legal scholar Glanville Williams considered this function to be the most important aspect of the legal response to youth offending. Glanville Williams advocated bringing children into a criminal justice system that was focussed more on the welfare of offenders than punishment. Glanville Williams argued that to divert young people from the criminal justice system 'saves the child not from prison, transportation, or the gallows, but from the probation officer, the foster-parents or the approved school' (Williams, 1954: 498).

International law also emphasises the importance of protecting the welfare of young people who engage in offending behaviour. The United Nations Convention on the Rights of the Child emphasises the need for states to develop a child-centred youth justice system in which the child's interests are paramount and the inherent dignity of the child is preserved. Article 3 of the United Nations Convention states that 'in all actions concerning children whether undertaken by public or private social welfare institutions, courts of law, administrative bodies or legislative bodies, the best interests of the child shall be the paramount consideration.' Furthermore Article 40 of the Convention on the Rights of the Child requires states to promote the 'dignity and worth' of any child alleged, accused or recognised as having committed a criminal offence. The United Nations Standard Minimum Rules for the Administration of Juvenile Justice (the Beijing Rules) 1985 recommend that every youth justice system should emphasise the well being of the young person. Article 52 of the United Nations Guidelines for the Prevention of Juvenile Delinquency (the Riyadh Guidelines) 1990 requires governments to enact laws that promote the well-being of all young people. Thus in England the state has a conventional obligation to safeguard and promote the best interests of its youngest citizens up to their 18th birthday, including those young people who have engaged in offending behaviour.

## Protecting the welfare of young offenders in the current youth justice system

From the 1970s onwards in England, there was a noticeable change in the tenor of official concern about the welfare of young people who engage in offending behaviour. As occurred in the USA, the symbolic image of the 'young offender' became ascendant and the lived reality of the 'child in need' was overshadowed. This stance set the tone for refocussing policy and practice in relation to children in trouble upon punishment, retribution and the wholesale incarceration of children. Although the Children and Young Persons Act 1969 gave primacy to the family and the social circumstances of the deprived and underprivileged and aimed to reduce the criminalisation of young people, large sections of the 1969 Act were never implemented and the welfare ideology underlying the Act never came to fruition. Juvenile courts continued to function largely as they had before, and though care proceedings following commission of an offence were made possible, such powers were used sparingly (Cavadino and Dignan, 2002; Harris, 1991). The Children Act 1989 removed from the juvenile court the power to order a young person into the care of a local authority. Sections 90(1) and (2) Children Act 1989 respectively repealed section 1(2)(f) and section 7(7) Children and Young Persons Act 1969. Care and supervision orders can now only be made in the Family Proceedings Court and only when it is proved that the child in question 'is suffering significant harm' and is 'beyond parental control'.

Section 1 of the Children Act 1989 requires that when a court determines any question with respect to the upbringing of a child, 'the child's welfare shall be the court's paramount consideration'. However, statutory *Guidance* states that this welfare principle only applies to proceedings under the 1989 Act (Department for Education and Skills, 2008: 1.9). Guidance does not carry the same legal force as the Statute or the Regulations. Nonetheless they are issued under section 7 of the Local Government (Social Services) Act 1970 and local authorities are required to act in accordance with such guidance, which is intended to be a statement of what is held to be good practice, and are likely to be quoted or used in court proceedings as well as in local authority policy and practice papers. They could provide the basis for a legal challenge of an authority's action or inaction. Thus it may be seen as a form of tertiary legislation. In *A v London Borough of Lambeth* ([2001] 2 FLR 1201, 1208) Scott Baker J observed that although *Guidance* does not determine the meaning of the Act it does give some insight into the way in which the Act was intended to operate. Likewise Sedley J pointed out in *R v Islington London Borough ex parte Rixon* ((1996) 1 CCLRep 119, 123) that local authorities are expected to follow the *Guidance* unless they can articulate a good reason for departing from it. Thus it would seem that the overarching welfare principle of the 1989 Act does not extend to provisions dealing with young offenders.

The advent of the 'New' Labour government in 1997 signalled the development of a more punitive approach in youth justice in which the welfare needs of young people who engage in anti-social and offending behaviour became marginalised, and more and more young people were brought within the criminal justice system for an ever-growing range of behaviour (Goldson, 2000a). The marginalisation of the young person's welfare needs was reflected in the White Paper *No More Excuses* which stated that 'punishment is necessary to signal society's disapproval when any person including a young person breaks the law . . . Young people . . . should be in no doubt about the tough penalties they will face . . . ' (Home Office, 1997a: 5.1). Section 37 of the Crime and Disorder Act 1998 places all those carrying out functions in relation to the youth justice system under a statutory duty to have regard to the principal aim of preventing offending by children and young people. The Crime and Disorder Act 1998 gives no direction to the courts or anyone else working in the youth justice system that the child's welfare should be of primary consideration. Consequently the primary duty of those involved in the youth justice system, including the police, is to prevent offending and not necessarily to promote the child's best interests (Hollingsworth, 2007a). This new aim of youth crime prevention signals a political preference for a punitive response to young people's behaviour (Pitts, 2001; Muncie, 2002) and potentially allows for welfare considerations to be circumvented. This aim allows for young people to be portrayed as threats to public safety and the youth justice system is cast in the role of preventing this threat being realised. In this representation, the young person's welfare needs can easily become a secondary concern (Smith, 2006: 97–8; Mason and Prior, 2008: 280).

Section 9 of the Criminal Justice and Immigration Act 2008 has elevated the aim of preventing offending and reoffending to the principal consideration when sentencing young offenders. In addition to the primary aim of preventing offending, the courts are required to have regard to the following

factors when sentencing: the punishment of offenders; the reform and rehabilitation of offenders; the protection of the public; and the making of reparation by offenders to the victims of their offences. Omitted from the list of
considerations which courts should have regard to when sentencing young
people are: the individual's age and vulnerability; evidence of the effectiveness of the proposed sentence; and what particular interventions have been
tried if the person has been sentenced before and what would be appropriate now. While the courts are required to have regard to the welfare of
the young person who has engaged in offending behaviour when sentencing,
in accordance with section 44 of the Children and Young Persons Act 1933,
section 9(3)(3) of the 2008 Act makes clear that welfare needs will not have
equal status, nor will they override the primary aim of preventing offending
(Bateman, 2007; Turner, 2007; Youth Justice Board, 2008a). Welfare
concerns are also ominously absent from the Youth Justice Board's Strategic
Objectives for 2008–2011, these objectives are to: prevent offending and
reoffending by children and young people under 18 years of age; to increase
victim and public confidence; and to ensure safe and effective use of
custody. (Youth Justice Board, 2008b). The most recent report of the
United Nations Committee on the Rights of the Child expressed regret that
the best interests of the child is still not reflected as a primary consideration
in youth justice law and recommended that the best interests principle be
integrated in all youth justice law and policy (United Nations Committee on
the Rights of the Child, 2008: 26–7).

## Welfare considerations in the Scottish youth justice system

The Scottish approach to youth offending provides a contemporary example
of the importance of protecting the best interests of young offenders and
the importance of recognising the connection between the difficult family
and social circumstances which beset not only young people in need but also
young people who offend. Scotland has one of the lowest ages of criminal
responsibility in Europe, 8 years of age, but the consequences of youth
offending are almost all framed within the welfare system. The origins of
the Scottish system of youth justice date back to the Report of the
Kilbrandon Committee (Kilbrandon, 1964). The Kilbrandon Committee
believed that in terms of the child's actual needs, the legal distinction
between young offenders and children in need of care or protection was
very often of little practical significance. Kilbrandon argued that more often
than not the problems of the child in need and the delinquent child can be
traced to shortcomings in the normal upbringing process in either the home,
the family environment or in the schools. Kilbrandon described such children, whether they were children in need or offenders, as 'hostages to
fortune'. It was considered essential to extend to this minority of children
the measures that their needs dictate and of which they have previously
been deprived.

In Scotland, the overriding and paramount principle is the welfare of the child and all decisions must be made in the interests of safeguarding that welfare (section 16 Children (Scotland) Act 1995). Cases are initially referred to a Reporter from a range of bodies including social work departments, the police and education authorities. The Reporter must decide whether referrals should be discharged with no further action or whether they should be referred to a social work department or to a children's hearing. The main grounds for referral to a children's hearing are that the child: is in need; has offended; has been offended against; has truanted; has misused drugs or alcohol; has been physically, emotionally or sexually abused; has fallen into bad associations; is in moral danger; needs care and protection; or the child is out of control (section 52 Children (Scotland) Act 1995). No distinction is made between children referred because of an allegation that an offence has been committed and the other grounds. When a case reaches a children's hearing it is deliberated upon by three lay panel members who are selected to be reasonably representative of the community in terms of age, ethnicity and occupational background. The hearing can only proceed if guilt is admitted. If a child or parent denies the commission of an offence then the case is referred to the Sheriff's court for the offence to be proved. If proved the child is referred back to the children's hearing. The children's hearing is solely concerned with deciding a future course of action and the welfare of the child is the paramount consideration in the decision making process (section 16 Children (Scotland) Act 1995). The hearing takes account of all aspects of a child's conduct, not simply the offence that has been committed. The panel considers many different facts in reaching its decision, including findings from social workers, school officials, children's homes and psychiatrists. The panel also considers what other people have done and neglected to do for the child. It recognises that the incident of an offence for which a child might be referred may only be one of several aspects involved in relation to a child's welfare.

The Scottish system has won praise throughout the world for the relaxed and informal way in which it deals with children who have committed crimes (Arthur, 2004; King, 1997; Whyte, 2003). The advantages of the Scottish youth justice system include its child-centeredness and its focus on welfare. The Scottish system adopts a holistic approach, looking beyond the deeds of young offenders and provides a multidisciplinary assessment of children under the age of 16 years. The Scottish system does not distinguish between troubled young people and young people in trouble. Indeed McGhee and Waterhouse found in their study of 482 children referred to the Scottish hearing system in February 1995 that 30 per cent of 'young offenders' first entered the system on a care and protection ground and that 29 per cent of 'non-offenders' first entered the system for committing an offence (McGhee and Waterhouse, 2007). These figures illustrate starkly that there is little to distinguish the young person who offends from the young person who is in need of adoption and guardianship or involved in access and custody disputes. Yet in England and Wales both groups of children are afforded varying levels of legal protection. The NCH Scotland reviewed the continuing relevance and fitness for purpose of the Scottish children's hearing system and concluded that this system offers a more humane and effective response to children in trouble than the response of the English youth justice system (NCH Scotland, 2004: 26). The NCH specifically discouraged adopting an increasingly punitive response in Scotland. This warning echoes the advice of the four UK Children's Commissioners in their combined report to the United Nations Committee on the Rights of the Child. The UK Children's Commissioners recommended that the best interests and welfare of the child should be a primary consideration in dealing with children in trouble with the law throughout the UK and that consideration should be given to adopting an improved Scottish welfare-based children's hearing system across the UK (United Kingdom Children's Commissioners, 2008: 173). Improvements could include, for example, raising the age of criminal responsibility in Scotland which at 8 years is the lowest in Europe. Similarly, by comparison with many European countries, the age of criminal majority in Scotland, at 16 years, is low. This contrasts with most European countries where the age of criminal majority is fixed at 18. Although children under 16 years are less likely to be punished by the courts, custody rates for 16 and 17 year olds are the highest in Europe (United Kingdom Children's Commissioners, 2008: 7).

## The welfare approach to tackling youth offending in other jurisdictions

Scotland is not the only country which adopts a welfare approach to tackling youth offending; such an approach is prevalent throughout Europe. For example, in France the vast majority of youth offending cases are usually referred to the 'juge des enfants' for social welfare support rather than puni-tive measures. The 'juge des enfants' investigates the young person's life in order to understand the reasons behind the offending behaviour. In France priority is placed on understanding the young person's actions and taking into consideration the personal situation of the juvenile in order to prevent offending, rather than condemning the child. Similarly in all Scandinavian countries young offenders under 18 years of age are subject to a system of justice that is geared mostly towards social services with incarceration as the last resort. For example, in Finland the offending behaviour of young people is managed within the child welfare system. This system is very clearly based on the assessment of the needs of trouble-making children, and offending youth are considered as being in need of supervision and control. In Denmark and Sweden when young people under 18 years of age commit offences the social welfare authorities intervene. Youth crime is seen as a social problem and young offenders are regarded as in need of protection and support. Therefore when the social welfare authorities make a decision regarding a suitable measure as a reaction to offending behaviour, the decision is based solely on the young person's social and family situation. Typical interventions include: meeting with a social worker; family therapy; or intermediate care, which involves structured activity with the young person in their home. In Norway, when children under 18 years commit an offence, the Child Welfare Service initiates measures pursuant to the Norwegian Child Welfare Act 1992. As far as possible voluntary preventive measures in the home will be used, such as providing the child with a mentor or helping the child to take part in meaningful leisure-time activities, or providing a home consultant who can counsel the parents on appropriate ways of relating to their child. Further measures may involve compulsory preventive help in the home, voluntary care in a foster home or an institution, compulsory out-of-home care, and as a last resort compulsory adoption. In Iceland, if the local Child Welfare Committee has reasonable grounds for suspecting that a child may harm his health or development through his behaviour, the Committee must institute an inquiry. The Child Welfare Committee must provide special support, in the form of guidance talks, counselling, placement in a home or an institution or other possible support measures, if a child is in fact endangering his health or development through his way of life, such as by engaging in crime or other similar harmful behaviour. In such circumstances, upon consultation with the parents, the Child Welfare Committee can also place the child in a suitable home or institution for treatment and examination.

In all of the jurisdictions examined above, the criminal justice system is not considered an appropriate response to a child's offences. Instead, responding to youth offending is seen in relation to a general concern for the mental and physical health of children as a means of promoting, in the long term, the mental and physical health of the community.

## Problems with a welfare approach to tackling youth offending

The welfare approach is characterised as diverting children from the system of criminal justice to a system based on treatment, care, protection and upholding the best interests of the child. The rights of the child are theoretically protected through the discretionary practices of experts and professionals who are qualified to judge how care might be exercised effectively in each case (Scraton and Haydon, 2002). Does this approach create any potential problems?

The discretion of experts and professionals, which allows treatment to be tailored to the particular needs of each child, is also vulnerable to subjective values, inconsistency, arbitrariness and prejudice along class, race and gender lines (Ferguson, 2007: 190). Asquith (1983) argues that the welfare approach lacks any clear and sound philosophical base, adequate legal and judicial safeguards, and transparency. Meeting the 'needs' of offenders has been considered as a spurious justification for placing excessive restrictions on individual liberty which are out of proportion either to the seriousness of the offence or to the realities of being in 'need of care and protection', and may in fact be subjecting young offenders to value-laden interventions (Reece, 1996). Social work interventions may also serve to undermine the right to natural justice. Young people may experience a sense of double jeopardy, sentenced for their background as well as for their offence. Welfarism has also been critiqued for encouraging state dependence, over-loading the responsibilities of the state and undermining the ability of individuals to take responsibility for their own actions (Muncie, 2005: 37–8).

In the English youth justice system welfare considerations have been marginalised. This approach has resulted in a youth justice system which criminalises children at an earlier age than most comparable countries and where considerably more is spent on locking up young people than on projects to prevent them engaging in offending behaviour. This has resulted in the charge that England and Wales is 'the site of the most punitive youth justice system in Europe' (Goldson and Muncie, 2006: ix). The English youth justice system overlooks the reality of the lives of young people who engage in offending behaviour, represents a serious diminution in the rights historically afforded to young people who offend, and also represents an abrogation of children's rights under the United Nations Convention on the Rights of the Child. The legal response to youth offending should reflect the evidence which proves that most young offender's have suffered vulnerable, abusive and disadvantaged lives. Young offenders are victims of deprived and depriving families and should be seen as under-socialised individuals in need of help and assistance. Both troubled and troublesome young people share the same characteristics and needs, therefore both groups deserve the same constitutional protection of their best interests. The English youth justice system should adopt a more welfare-orientated approach to tackling youth offending. Smith recommends that we should reinsert a proper concern with the 'welfare' principle that has been crowded out of the youth justice system and thus develop an intervention strategy that is based on dealing with young people holistically and considering the factors underlying the offence (Smith, 2007: 227). One way of making this argument more compelling is to draw attention to the evidence which shows that countries that invest in universal welfare provisions tend to have the lowest levels of penal custody (Downes and Hansen, 2006). Thus investment in, and commitment to, protecting the welfare concerns of all young people, including young offenders, can be cost effective in the long term. Such a commitment to protecting the welfare of young people who offend would also help to create a youth justice system which addresses the root causes of youth offending rather than one which is committed to criminalising and incarcerating increasing numbers of young people.

## Discussion topic

Examine the rise and fall of welfarism as a feature of the youth justice system

## *Comment*

Since the nineteenth century the principles of acting in a child's best interests and making welfare considerations a paramount concern in court proceedings have underpinned the development of youth justice systems throughout the world. From the 1970s there was a notable shift from a welfare model based on meeting individual needs to a justice model more concerned with the offence than the offender. At the beginning of the twenty-first century, in the English youth justice system welfare considerations have been marginalised and replaced by the central aim of youth crime prevention. This approach has resulted in a youth justice system which criminalises children at an earlier age than most comparable countries and where considerably more is spent on locking up young people than on projects to prevent them engaging in offending behaviour.

## Suggested further reading

Bottoms, A. (2002) 'On the decriminalisation of English juvenile courts' in Muncie, J., Hughes, G. and McLaughlin, E. *Youth Justice Critical Readings*, London: Sage, pp. 216–27.

Hollingsworth, K. (2007) 'Judicial approaches to children's rights in youth crime', *Child and Family Law Quarterly*, 19, 1, 42.

McGhee, J. and Waterhouse, L. (2007) 'Classification in youth justice and child welfare: in search of 'the child', *Youth Justice*, 7(2), 107–20.

# 7    Preventing youth offending

## Introduction

As seen in the previous chapter, the advent of the 'New' Labour government in May 1997 signalled an increasing recognition of the determination to prevent youth offending. Both the Crime and Disorder Act 1998 and the Criminal Justice and Immigration Act 2008 place the prevention of youth offending as the principal aim of youth justice law and policy. This chapter will examine the development and impact of the emphasis on youth crime prevention on how youth justice services are delivered. This chapter will also consider whether the emphasis on preventing youth offending conflicts with the need to protect the welfare of all young people, including those young people who engage in offending behaviour.

## Legal obligation to prevent youth offending in the English youth justice system: the Crime and Disorder Act 1998

Section 37 of the Crime and Disorder Act 1998 places all those carrying out functions in relation to the youth justice system under a statutory duty to have regard to the principal aim of preventing offending by children and young people. In the White Paper *No More Excuses* the government stressed that it did not see any conflict between protecting the welfare of the young offender and preventing that individual from offending again, 'preventing offending promotes the welfare of the individual young offender and protects the public' (Home Office, 1997a: 2.2).

The Crime and Disorder Act 1998 created youth offending teams in order to help achieve the ambitious aim of preventing youth offending. The youth offending team (YOT) comprises representatives from the police, probation, education and health authorities and the local authority, thus guaranteeing that teams of trained professionals with specific disciplines work together to tackle youth offending. The YOT works with young people aged 10–17 who are offending or at risk of offending, as well as those under 10, in order to prevent offending. The YOT has primary responsibility for coordinating youth justice services across a geographical area, providing a multi-agency service for children and young people at risk of offending, or who are involved in offending behaviour, and carrying out such functions as are assigned to them in the Youth Justice Plan formulated by the local authority (section 41 Crime and Disorder Act 1998). The youth crime prevention role of the YOT is underlined by the Youth Justice Board's stated twin objectives of reducing the number of young people who offend and ensuring that young people most at risk of offending are targeted by mainstream services (Youth Justice Board, 2002a). The YOTs aim to deliver a wide range of programmes that tackle offending behaviour at the different stages of its development. YOTs have taken the lead in creating schemes to provide purposeful and engaging activities for young people at risk of offending. Examples of such schemes are described below.

## Youth Inclusion Programme

The Youth Inclusion Programme (YIP) works with young people who are most at risk of offending either due to poor family support, lack of schooling or low self-esteem. YIPs put in place a structured and supervised environment to provide an alternative activity for young people who might otherwise become involved in crime. The Youth Inclusion Programme is expected to target their work on the 50 most 'at risk' young people aged 13–16 in some of the most deprived neighbourhoods in the country. This group of young people are identified through a multi-agency consultation process, drawing on input from the youth offending team, police, local authority social services, education or schools, other local agencies and the community. While projects are intended to target the most 'at risk' young people in each area, they are also required to serve all young people in their neighbourhood; indeed the inclusive nature of project activities are central to their success in enrolling 'difficult to reach' young people. Participation is therefore voluntary and any teenager who wants to can join, as the aim is to provide somewhere safe for young people to go where they learn new skills, take part in sporting or other activities, and benefit from educational support. The YIPs cover a broad range of preventive measures, including: after-school activities; teaching basic skills; life/social skills development such as drug and sex education and activities designed to teach relationship skills; youth work; mentoring; environmental work and recreation. Team sports, debating society and creative classes aim to teach young people the value of working together, listening, cooperating with others and building self-esteem. Spending time with the positive role models of workers and volunteer mentors can help change young people's attitude to crime.

## Positive activities for young people

School holidays are traditionally considered a prime time for young people to become involved in anti-social or criminal behaviour. The absence of a structured day and in many cases the absence of a responsible adult to supervise their activities results in an increase in youth offending. The purpose of the Positive Activities for Young People scheme is to reduce this offending in high crime areas by engaging 13–17 year olds in constructive activities during the daytime when they may otherwise be unoccupied and thus at risk of engaging in offending behaviour. Each Positive Activities for Young People scheme provides five weeks of activity engaging at least 100 young people, including a core group of 13–17 year olds most at risk of offending. A multifaceted referral process is adopted through which formal referrals are sought from a number of agencies, including schools, youth offending teams, police, housing departments and local authority social service departments. Otherwise referrals are on a broad self-referral neighbourhood basis. Activities range from reading and writing skills to sport, art, dance, computer skills, life skills, vocational skills as well as having talks on the realities of prison, health, substance misuse and sex education. Using this approach, the programmes aim to assist young people and their families to minimise the causal factors associated with involvement in youth crime and anti-social behaviour.

## Mentoring programmes

Many young offenders lack a stable adult presence in their lives: someone who is prepared to provide them with the advice and support they need as they face the challenges of growing up. By training and supporting adults to form relationships with young people who are at risk of offending, or those who have offended, YOTs can provide a healthy role model, sometimes for the first time in a young person's life. Such mentors can show young people that there are alternatives to offending. Mentors are expected to offer advice on key areas of the young person's life such as family issues, education and training.

Youth offending teams are capable of acting speedily and effectively to prevent young people from offending by providing help with their physical and mental well-being and any family problems they are experiencing. The United Nations Committee on the Rights of the Child welcomed the creation of these multidisciplinary teams to respond to youth offending behaviour (United Nations Committee on the Rights of the Child, 2002: 59). Youth offending teams offer a large selection of youth crime prevention programmes which could prove to be a valuable and effective resource in helping local authorities to exercise their youth crime prevention functions. In addition to creating YOTs, the Crime and Disorder Act 1998 also gives local authorities a number of new and novel powers in relation to preventing young people from engaging in offending behaviour by providing powers for targeted early interventions with young children at risk of offending, rather than reacting to criminal conduct after if has been committed. Such powers include the child safety order, the child curfew scheme and the anti-social behaviour order.

## Child safety order

A local authority may apply for a child safety order under section 11 of the Crime and Disorder Act 1998. The child safety order is designed to protect children under 10 who are at risk of becoming involved in crime or who have already started to behave in an anti-social or criminal manner (Home Office 1997b: 5.5). The child safety order is represented as a measure designed to prevent children being drawn into crime by providing an opportunity to intervene positively to protect the young person's welfare (United Kingdom Government, 1999). If a magistrates court, upon the application of a local authority, is satisfied that one or more of the conditions, outlined below, are fulfilled with respect to a child under the age of 10, then it may make a child safety order (section 11(1) Crime and Disorder Act 1998). The conditions are that:

(a) the child has committed an act which, if he had been aged 10 or over would constitute an offence;
(b) a child safety order is necessary for the purpose of preventing the commission by the child of such an act as described in (a);
(c) the child has contravened a ban imposed by a curfew order;
(d) the child has acted in a manner that has caused, or was likely to cause harassment, alarm or distress to two or more persons not of the same household as the young person.

It would appear from these conditions that the order can be made before any act of criminality has occurred (Hayes 1999; Vaughan 2000). The child safety order places the child under the supervision of the responsible officer (either a social worker from a local authority social services department or a member of a youth offending team) and requires the child to comply with such requirements as are specified in section 11 of Crime and Disorder Act 1998. Section 11 provides that the court may specify such requirements as are considered desirable in the interest of securing that the child receives appropriate care, protection and support, and is subject to proper control for the purpose of preventing any repetition of the kind of behaviour which led to the order being made in the first place. Failure to comply with the order will leave the way open for local authorities to commence care proceedings under the Children Act 1989. In these circumstances the threshold criteria of the Children Act 1989 do not have to be satisfied (section 12(7) Crime and Disorder Act 1998). The standard of proof applicable to child safety order proceedings is that of civil proceedings (section 11(6) Crime and Disorder Act 1998). Hence the order appears to act in a similar vein to a supervision order under section 31 of the Children Act 1989. However the important difference between both these orders is that the maximum duration of the child safety order is three months, unless the circumstances necessitate an extension to a total of twelve months (section

11(3) Crime and Disorder Act 1998). By contrast, a supervision order under the Children Act 1989 will last for twelve months with further extensions possible to a maximum of three years.

The Child Safety Order is founded on the belief that early intervention is more effective than waiting until the child is old enough to be dealt with under the youth justice system (Hayes, 1999: 318) and that the order will prevent 'children slipping into the criminal habit' (Home Office, 1997b: 102). Part of the thinking informing child safety orders is protective of children: responsible adults normally take the view that young children should not be out late at night and should not be involved in offending behaviour. Thus the order supplements the existing welfare provisions available under the Children Act 1989 by providing an opportunity to intervene positively to protect the welfare of a child who appears to be at risk of becoming involved in crime (Home Office, 2000). By emphasising the parental role within youth crime, whether it be from a point of lack of control, or simply lack of interest, responsibility for crime is clearly being placed not just on the individual, but within the family unit. However a consequence of the child safety order is that children under 10 years of age who have committed, or might commit, offences will be penalised, despite the fact that children under the age of 10 years are below the age of criminal responsibility and accordingly are not considered to be capable of committing criminal offences. Thus it appears somewhat anomalous that the child should be held accountable within the civil jurisdiction. Fionda believes that the aim of the child safety order is 'to abandon the minimum age of criminal responsibility without stirring up the political hornets' nest that would have ensued had they done so expressly' (Fionda, 1999: 45). It is also questionable whether punitive orders are the best means of controlling children under 10 years and preventing them from offending or behaving disruptively. It may well be more productive to increase the resources and funding for family support services for children in need and their families.

## Child curfew scheme

To enable the local authority to prevent crime by young people, section 14(1) of the Crime and Disorder Act 1998 allows a local authority to implement a child curfew scheme. Such a scheme creates a ban on all children under the age of 10 years being in a public place within a specified area during specified hours and otherwise than under the effective control of a responsible person aged 18 years or over (section 14(2) Crime and Disorder Act 1998). Child curfews are aimed at preventing unsupervised children gathering in public places at night and causing 'alarm or misery to local communities' (United Kingdom Government, 1999). Sections 48 and 49 of the Criminal Justice and Police Act 2001 raised the age limit of child curfew schemes to cover unsupervised children up to and including the age of 15 years. The 2001 Act also allows Chief Officers of Police, as well as local authorities, to apply for a child curfew scheme. Local child curfew schemes are designed with the dual aim of maintaining order and of protecting the local community from the alarm and distress caused by groups of young people involved in anti-social behaviour at night and also to protect young children who, because they are on the streets unsupervised, may be at risk of harm or of engaging in offending behaviour. Local authorities can impose these curfews on the basis that such children are at risk of engaging in offending behaviour. There is no criminal penalty for any child found in breach of the curfew order; it is designed solely to protect children and reduce the risk of them offending and behaving anti-socially (Home Office, 2001). Where a child is found in breach of a curfew, the local authority must be informed and must, as soon as practicable, investigate the reasons for the breach. This investigation may reveal a need for support services under the Children Act 1989, or breach of the curfew may constitute sufficient grounds for the imposition of a child safety order.

Because the order can be made even where children in the area concerned have committed no offence, it is arguable that this order penalises the normal behaviour of ordinary children who are hanging about on the streets (Gelsthorpe and Morris, 1999: 215). This may be one of the reasons why local authorities have been reluctant to apply for curfew orders. The Anti-Social Behaviour Act 2003 aimed to overcome this reluctance by providing police with the power to disperse people of any age from being in a particular area for up to 24 hours. Section 30 of the 2003 Act can be invoked where any member of the public has been intimidated, harassed, alarmed or distressed by the presence or behaviour of a group of two or more people in a public place. The anti-social behaviour must be significant and persistent.

## Anti-social behaviour order (ASBO)

Section 1(1) of the Crime and Disorder Act 1998 allows relevant authorities (namely the local authority or the police) to apply to the magistrates court for an anti-social behaviour order (ASBO), if it appears to the authority that the following conditions are fulfilled with respect to any person aged 10 or over, namely:

(a) that the person has acted in an anti-social manner, that is to say in a manner that caused, or was likely to cause harassment, alarm or distress to one or more persons not of the same household; and
(b) that such an order is necessary to protect persons in the local government area in which the harassment, alarm or distress was caused or was likely to be caused from further anti-social acts by the young person.

Acting in an anti-social manner is defined as acting in a manner that caused or was likely to cause alarm or distress, and includes behaviour that puts people in fear of crime (section 19(1)(a) Crime and Disorder Act 1998). The Solicitor-General expanded upon this definition by maintaining that the anti-social behaviour order is intended to deal with behaviour that is 'so intrusive as to make a real, unpleasant impact on neighbours and others affected . . . ' (cited in Rutherford, 1998: 14). Statutory guidance on the use of ASBOs states that there is no requirement to prove that the accused intended to cause alarm or distress (Home Office, 1999), which effectively removes the requirement for *mens rea*. This definition of anti-social behaviour allows for local authorities to adapt a flexible, ambiguous and inconsistent approach in applying for and administering ASBOs (Donoghue, 2007: 418) The European Commissioner for Human Rights believes that the determination of what constitutes anti-social behaviour has become 'conditional upon the subjective views of any given collective' (Gil-Robles, 2005: 34). Other commentators have suggested that the definition of anti-social behaviour 'is only limited by one person's imagination' (Black, 2005) and can mean 'whatever the victim says it means' (Chakrabarti, 2006: 23).

The aim of the ASBO is to target the anti-social behaviour of those aged 10 years and over. An individual complainant cannot apply to a magistrates court for an anti-social behaviour order. If an individual considers that there is a need for an order they will need to make a representation to the local authority or the police. If neither of these bodies decides to seek an anti-social behaviour order the individual may seek to challenge the decision not to proceed by an application for judicial review. An anti-social behaviour order prohibits the defendant from doing anything described in the order. The order lasts for a period of not less than two years and can only prohibit conduct; it cannot specify positive acts to be done. Breach of the order is a criminal offence punishable by a fine and/or imprisonment for up to five years (section 10 Crime and Disorder Act 1998). In *R v Manchester Crown Court, ex parte McCann and Ors* ([2001] 1 WLR 358) the Court of Appeal held that proceedings to obtain an anti-social behaviour order were civil and not subject to the stricter criminal rules of evidence. The court must decide on the balance of probabilities, whether the accused has behaved in an anti-social manner and that an order is needed to protect the public from further anti-social behaviour This decision also stated that the standard of proof is flexible, to be applied with greater or lesser strictness according to the seriousness of what has to be proved. The court concluded that the categorisation of an application for an anti-social behaviour order as a civil matter did not create an infringement of the Human Rights Act 1998. A breach of an ASBO could lead to the young person being incarcerated, sometimes for conduct which by itself would not result in such a severe punishment. ASBOs criminalise sub-criminal behaviour where breach of civil law and lower standards of proof are punishable with custodial sentences. As the European Commissioner for Human Rights observed, 'such orders look rather like personalised penal codes, where non-criminal behaviour becomes criminal for individuals who have incurred the wrath of the community' (Gil-Robles, 2005: 34).

The Police Reform Act 2002 allows local authorities or the police to apply for an interim anti-social behaviour order to stop anti-social and offending behaviour at the earliest stage possible. Alternatively young people engaging in, or at risk of engaging in, anti-social behaviour may be asked to sign an acceptable behaviour contract (ABC). An ABC is an individually written agreement by a young person with the police and a partner agency, such as the local authority, youth offending team or school, not to carry on with anti-social conduct such as harassment, graffiti, criminal damage and verbal abuse. Acceptable behaviour contracts are flexible in terms of content and format and provide an effective means of encouraging children and parents to take responsibility for unacceptable behaviour. Anti-social behaviour orders and acceptable behaviour contracts are designed to both deter future anti-social behaviour and to prevent escalation of existing behaviour, without having to resort to criminal sanctions (Campbell, 2002; Collins, 2001). These orders are powerful tools for local authorities in their attempts to reduce crime and anti-social behaviour, as they enable local authorities to intervene to prevent anti-social and offending behaviour by children aged 10 years and above who are considered at risk of offending. The Criminal Justice Act 2003 introduced an innovative new individual support order (ISO) (section 322 Criminal Justice Act 2003). The ISO extends the protection that ASBOs provide to the community by requiring children and young people with ASBOs to undertake individually tailored activities, such as attending treatment for substance abuse. The aim is to improve the effectiveness of an ASBO by engaging the child or young person in addressing the root causes of their actions and aiming to solve these problems.

The draft guidance document on the use of the ASBO, circulated for consultation soon after the Crime and Disorder Act was passed, suggested that the use of ASBOs in relation to children and young people should be considered 'in the context of wider work to prevent crime and disorder among that age group' (Home Office, 1998b: 3.5). ASBOs tend to be used against young people who engage in the most serious forms of anti-social behaviour and who have a long history of criminality (Campbell, 2002). Amongst this group of young people, ASBOs may be seen as a 'badge of honour' and the publicity they receive glamorises their criminal status (Willow, 2005). In fact, labelling a person as deviant makes it difficult for the young person to overcome this label and may encourage the young person to embrace their new identity (Hodgkinson and Tilley, 2007).

The Crime and Disorder Act 1998 has introduced a considerable range of initiatives intended to discourage youth anti-social and offending behaviour, together with a growing understanding of the parameters and requirements of appropriate provision to meet the individual needs of parents and diversity of family life. All of the orders contained in the 1998 Act aim to reinforce parental responsibility and prevent young children, including those under the age of 10 years, from slipping into criminal ways. What is significant about all of these measures is that they do not depend upon a criminal offence being committed had the child been 10 years or older; it is sufficient that the local community deems the behaviour disruptive or that the child is judged to be at risk of committing a criminal offence.

## Legal obligation to prevent youth offending in the English youth justice system: the Criminal Justice and Immigration Act 2008 and the Children Act 1989

The aim of youth crime prevention is also expressed in other legislation. Section 9 of the Criminal Justice and Immigration Act 2008 has elevated the aim of preventing offending and reoffending to the principal consideration of the youth court when sentencing young offenders. The 2008 Act requires the court to have regard to the following factors when sentencing young people: the principle aim of the youth justice system; the welfare of the offender; and the purposes of sentencing. The purposes of sentencing include punishment, reform and rehabilitation, protection of the public and reparation (section 142A(3) Criminal Justice and Immigration Act 2008). No advice is provided as to which of these factors should take priority in the case of a conflict amongst them. In the Youth Crime Action Plan 2008 the government states the principle that when young people are found guilty of a crime they should receive a sentence which protects the public and punishes the offender, but which also aims to prevent further offending.

Increasing recognition of the potential role of local authorities in preventing delinquency and youth offending has also been reflected in legislation prior to the Crime and Disorder Act 1998. Schedule 2 of the Children Act 1989 requires local authorities to take reasonable steps to encourage children in their area not to commit criminal offences. *Guidance* suggests that, in addition to intermediate treatment for those at risk of offending and the supervision of young offenders, this might involve: advice and support services for parents; the provision of family support services; family centres, day care and accommodation; and ensuring that children in need gain maximum life benefits from educational opportunities, health care and social care leading to reduced rates of offending by such children (Department of Health, 1991). Hence the Children Act 1989 recognises that the local authority's duty to assist children in need is directly connected to their responsibility for preventing youthful offending behaviour, thus the relevance of family support systems to delinquency and crime prevention is acknowledged. The government's Green Paper *Every Child Matters* (Chief Secretary to the Treasury, 2003) sets out a comprehensive framework in which universal services such as schools, health services, family support and child care should provide help and information to families, especially at key transition points in their children's lives. Among the many objectives of the

Green Paper was that of reducing the number of children engaged in offending or anti-social behaviour. *Every Child Matters* proposed the strengthening of preventive services for children by focusing on four key themes: (a) supporting families and carers; (b) ensuring necessary intervention before children reach crisis point and protecting children from falling through the net; (c) addressing underlying problems such as weak accountability and poor service integration; and (d) ensuring that people working with children are trained, valued and rewarded. The Children Act 2004 provides the statutory underpinning for *Every Child Matters*. The Children Act 2004 enshrines in law the ambition that all local authorities in England shall establish children's trusts. The 2004 Act places key agencies, including YOTs, under a new duty to cooperate with local authorities and other agencies to promote positive outcomes for children However, to what extent the YOTs should be incorporated into children's trusts arrangements has largely been left to local discretion. *Youth Justice – the Next Steps*, the companion document to *Every Child Matters*, showed little appetite for integrating youth justice services into mainstream children's services (Home Office, 2003). Similarly *Working Together to Safeguard Children 2006* aimed to provide statutory guidance to organisations on how they should work together to safeguard and promote the welfare of children (Department for Education and Skills, 2006). However, this document offers no advice on working together to prevent youth anti-social and offending behaviour.

## The impact of the youth crime prevention aim on the youth justice system

Solomon and Garside assessed the reforms to the English youth justice system since 1997 and considered the extent to which the government achieved its ambitious aim of preventing youth offending (Solomon and Garside, 2008). Solomon and Garside found that despite a substantial increase in spending the principal aim of the youth justice system to 'prevent offending by children and young persons' has yet to be achieved in any significant sense (Solomon and Garside, 2008: 65). Instead, the number of children in custody in England and Wales has risen to the highest number of children imprisoned in Western Europe (Council of Europe, 2004). The United Nations Committee on the Rights of the Child highlighted that youth custody in England and Wales was so high because detention is not always applied as a measure of last resort, as required by Article 37 of the UN Convention (United Nations Committee on the Rights of the Child, 2008: 77). A consequence of this approach to youth custody is that most of the Youth Justice Board's spending (64 per cent) purchases custodial places for children, ensuring that 10 times more is spent on custody than on prevention (Margo and Stevens, 2008: 5; Solomon and Garside, 2008: 9). The effect of this budget allocation is that the youth crime prevention schemes devised by youth offending teams are being developed and implemented in a piecemeal and incremental fashion. As a result of lack of resources and over-reliance on short-term funding, effective procedures for the establishment of social programmes to provide necessary support for children at risk of engaging in offending behaviour and their families are not being adequately developed.

In addition to preventing youth offending, youth offending teams have many statutory duties to fulfil, for example they are required to coordinate the provision of youth justice services for those in the area who need them (section 38(4) Crime and Disorder Act 1998). This includes: the provision of appropriate adult services under the Crime and Disorder Act final warning scheme provisions (section 65 Crime and Disorder Act 1998); assessment and intervention work in support of final warnings given by the police to young people who admit offending; the prompt provision of pre-sentence reports required by courts in criminal proceedings against young people; participation on youth offender panels; preparation of youth offender contracts; supervision of young people sentenced to a community sentence; coordination and provision of effective support for young people on bail; through care and post-release supervision for young people sentenced to a detention and training order or other custodial sentence. Thus much of the youth offending teams' core work is with known offenders and it is a matter for local decision how far YOTs are involved in preventing offending by young people who have not yet committed offences (Home Office *et al.* 1998: 32). Evidence suggests that much of the work of youth offending teams is concerned with those young people who have come to the notice of the criminal justice system and that preventing youth crime is a low priority (Wiles *et al.*, 1999). Gray found in her study of young people supervised by YOTs that YOTs appear to be playing the roles of prosecutor, enforcer, monitor and correctional mentor rather than adviser, mediator, advocator and counsellor. Gray found relatively little mediation between young people, their families and their schools. Gray's findings suggest that YOTs are providing little help in terms of social support to establish stable family relations, resolve health issues, and succeed in education, training and employment (Gray, 2005).

The UK Children's Commissioners, in their combined report to the United Nations Committee on the Rights of the Child, expressed concerns about the very punitive approach to misbehaviour by children and young people in England and Wales and the high numbers of children locked up (United Kingdom Children's Commissioners, 2008). The Commissioners were concerned that the principle of primary consideration for the best interests of the child is not being applied to children involved in the youth justice system in England and Wales. The Report estimated that between 2002 and 2006, crime committed by children fell, yet during the same period, it estimated that there was a 26 per cent increase in the number of children criminalised and prosecuted. The Commissioners were also concerned that custody is not being used as a last resort in England and Wales. The

Commissioners drew attention to the Scottish youth justice system which is less punitive and where imprisonment for young people under 16 years of age is far less common. In Scotland, until the age of 16 years, the youth justice system is focussed on the child's best interests and children are much less likely to be punished or locked up than in England.

It is noteworthy that in England and Wales the objective of section 37 of the Crime and Disorder Act 1998 appears to give priority to the prevention of offending by young people generally, and not necessarily by the individual offender. Thus a court may need to impose a deterrent sentence with the aim of preventing young people from offending, but which does not necessarily serve the welfare of the individual offender. This view is illustrated in the case of *R v Inner London Crown Court, ex p N. and S.* ([2001] 1 Cr App R 343). Two youths aged 16 and 17 years sought a judicial review of the Crown Court's dismissal of their appeals against sentences of four months Detention and Training Order for using threatening words and behaviour. Rose LJ examined section 37 of the Crime and Disorder Act 1998 and stated that the need to impose a deterrent sentence may take priority over the provisions of section 44(1) of the Children and Young Persons Act 1933 which requires the court to promote the welfare of individual offenders. Thus despite the government's assurances in *No More Excuses* to protect the welfare of young people who engage in offending behaviour, section 37 of the 1998 Act ignores the potentially corrosive impact of custodial life upon a young person's development (Stone, 2001).

The White Paper *No More Excuses* claimed that:

> [t]he United Kingdom is committed to protecting the welfare of children and young people who come into contact with the criminal justice process. The government does not accept that there is any conflict between protecting the welfare of the young offender and preventing that individual from offending again. Preventing offending promotes the welfare of the individual young offender and protects the public.
>
> (Home Office, 1997a: 2.2)

It is evident that a considerable range of initiatives intended to discourage juvenile anti-social and offending behaviour have been introduced, together with a growing understanding of the parameters and requirements of appropriate provision to meet the individual and diverse needs of young people who engage in anti-social and offending behaviour. However the views express in *No More Excuses* overlooks the reality that detention and retributive punishment have always occupied a central place in the control of young offenders. Evidence shows that prosecuting young people has no beneficial effect in preventing offending (Kemp *et al.*, 2002). A court appearance is as likely to confirm and extend an adolescent's deviant behaviour as it is to curb a delinquent career (Whyte, 2009). Thus the primacy afforded to prevention cannot be easily balanced with the need for the protection of the welfare of young people who engage in offending behaviour.

---

### Discussion topic

How has the aim of youth crime prevention impacted upon the delivery of contemporary youth justice?

---

### Comment

Since 1997 prevention has become a major feature of new policies and initiatives concerning children and their families. Accordingly there has been considerable investment in the Youth Justice Board and the 156 youth offending teams. They have benefited from larger real-terms growth in funding than any of the other criminal justice agencies, apart from probation. However the promotion of youth crime prevention as the central aim of youth justice policy has allowed the youth justice system in England and Wales to develop into a formal and rigid system which draws younger children into contact with the youth justice system and escalates them up the sentencing ladder and into custody. Protecting the welfare of the child now takes a lower priority than the aim of youth crime prevention. The number of children in custody in England and Wales has risen to the highest number of children imprisoned in Western Europe.

### Suggested further reading

Ashford, B. (2007) *Towards a Youth Crime Prevention Strategy*, London: Youth Justice Board.

Howe, R.B. (2008) 'Children's rights as crime prevention', *International Journal of Children's Rights*, 16, 4, 457–74.

Muncie, J. (2009) *Youth and Crime 3rd edn*, London: Sage, pp. 307–47.

# Part III

# The English youth justice system in practice

# 8 The role of the police and the youth court in tackling youth offending

## Introduction

Chapter 8 will examine the role of the police in tackling youth offending. The police will usually be the first to respond to offending by young people and they have a range of options which they can use to address youth offending, including reprimands, final warnings and youth conditional cautions. The police also have the power to charge a young person with committing an offence and refer them to the youth court for trial. This chapter will also examine the powers and functions of the youth court.

## Powers of the police

The powers and conduct of the police are largely regulated by the Police and Criminal Evidence Act 1984 (PACE). The Police and Criminal Evidence Act 1984 and associated Codes of Practice A to G govern the entire process of a criminal investigation from first encounter to the point of charge. PACE Code of Practice C pays particular attention to the position of children and young people as it concerns the codes of practice for the detention, treatment and questioning of people by the police. Code C treats as children all young people under 17 years of age. At 17 years, and not 18 years, at the police station the child is treated as an adult, and thus will not be entitled to any of the special protections afforded to young people. However if the child is sent to court, the child will appear as a youth in the youth court, and not the adult court.

## Powers of stop, search and arrest

The legal provisions regulating stop and search of young people are essentially the same as for adults. The police can stop and search any person or vehicle provided they have reasonable grounds for suspecting that they will find stolen goods or prohibited articles, for example drugs, an offensive weapon, knives or items which could damage or destroy property (section 1 Police and Criminal Evidence Act 1984). Thus police officers can only stop and search a person or vehicle where they have reasonable grounds for suspecting that they will find stolen or prohibited goods, unless a serious violent incident has taken place or if they believe it is necessary to prevent terrorism. In *Castorina v Chief Constable of Surrey* ((1988) 138 NLJ 180) the court held that 'reasonable grounds is objective and has nothing to do with the officer's state of mind'. The general powers of arrest are derived from common law principles and codified in the Police and Criminal Evidence Act 1984. The basis for a lawful arrest is 'reasonable suspicion' that an arrestable offence has been committed. Code A of PACE provides guidance on what 'reasonable suspicion' means. Reasonable suspicion can never be supported on the basis of personal factors alone without reliable supporting evidence. The phrase is given further clarification in Code G, paragraph.2:

> There must be some reasonable objective grounds for the suspicion, based on known facts or information which are relevant to the likelihood the offence has been committed and the person to be questioned committed it.

Thus police cannot stop, search and arrest based solely on factors such as race, age, stereotypes, failure to answer questions or previous criminal records.

## Arrival at the police station

On arrival at the police station, the custody officer must give the young person a written notice setting out their rights including: the right to have someone informed of the arrest; the right to consult privately with a solicitor available free of charge; and the right to consult the Code of Practice. Section 34 of the Children and Young Persons Act 1933 requires that where a young person under 17 years of age is in police detention, the parent or guardian must be informed as soon as practicable that their child has been arrested, why the child has been arrested and where the child is being detained. All of these rights can be delayed if exercising them may lead to interference or harm to evidence connected with an offence or interference and injury to any other person. Similarly these rights can be delayed if exercising them would lead to the alerting of other persons suspected in having committed such an offence, but not yet arrested for it; or hinder the removing of any property obtained as a result of such an offence (section 56(5) PACE 1984).

## Appropriate adult

All young people in police custody must be provided with an appropriate adult. In the case of a young person the 'appropriate adult' means:

(a)  a parent or guardian; or
(b)  a social worker of a local authority: or
(c)  failing either of the above, another responsible adult aged 18 years or over who is not a police officer or employed by the police.

A person, including a parent, should not be the appropriate adult if they are suspected of involvement in the offence, is the victim, is a witness or is involved in the investigation. If the parent or guardian is estranged from the young person they should not be asked to be the appropriate adult if the young person expressly objects. If a child in care admits an offence to a social worker then another social worker should be the appropriate adult. When a police officer detains a young person, the custody officer must, as soon as practicable, inform the appropriate adult of the grounds for the young person's detention and their whereabouts and ask the adult to come to the station to see the young person. It is irrelevant that the young person is able to understand procedures and answer questions; this does not diminish the need for an appropriate adult to assist, guide and protect the young person. If an appropriate adult is present at the interview they should be informed that they are not expected to act simply as an observer. The purpose of their presence is to: (a) advise the person being interviewed; (b) to observe whether or not the interview is being carried out fairly and properly; and (c) to facilitate communication with the person being interviewed (Code of Practice C, 11.17). The main concern of the appropriate adult is not establishing the innocence or guilt of the young person, but to ensure the protection of the child's physical, mental and emotional welfare.

A young person must not be interviewed regarding their involvement or suspected involvement in a criminal offence or be asked to provide or sign a written statement under caution or record of an interview in the absence of an appropriate adult, unless it is an urgent interview authorised by a superintendent. An interview can only occur in the absence of an appropriate adult if an officer of superintendent rank or above considers that a delay will: (a) involve a risk of harm to persons or serious loss or damage to property; (b) delay unnecessarily the person's release from custody; or (c) otherwise prejudice the investigation. If a young person is cautioned in the absence of an appropriate adult the caution must be repeated in the appropriate adult's presence.

Section 58 of the Police and Criminal Evidence Act 1984 (PACE) provides that a person arrested and held in police custody is entitled, if they so request, to consult a solicitor privately at any time. In the case of a young person, an appropriate adult should consider whether legal advice from a solicitor is required. In *R v Aspinall* ([1999] 2 Cr App R 115) it was held that a significant part of the duty of the appropriate adult was to advise about the presence of a solicitor at any questioning of the young person. The court held that the appropriate adult must aim to persuade the young person to exercise their right to legal advice by explaining the importance of legal advice. If the young person does not believe that legal advice is necessary, the appropriate adult has the right to ask for a solicitor to attend if this is in the best interests of the young person. However, the young person cannot be forced to speak with the solicitor if they do not wish to do so. The child must be given an opportunity to consult with the solicitor without the appropriate adult being present. This is important as the appropriate adult is not covered by legal privilege. Legal privilege protects confidential communications between solicitors and their clients for the purposes of giving and obtaining legal advice. On the other hand, a social worker or an appropriate adult may be bound to reveal information, when asked, which would lead to the prevention or detection of a crime.

Note 11C of the Detention Code states that 'special care should always be taken when questioning' young people as young people are prone to providing information which is unreliable, misleading or self-incriminatory. Young people are particularly susceptible to suggestive interrogation and 'are very keen to be released at almost any cost as soon as possible' (Littlechild, 1998: 8). It is important to obtain corroboration of any facts admitted wherever possible. Young people should not be arrested at their place of education unless this is unavoidable. If this occurs the school principal must be informed. Young people may only be interviewed at their place of education in exceptional circumstances and then only when the principal agrees and is present.

## Detention in a police station

Detention is only permissible to secure or preserve evidence or obtain evidence by questioning. The custody officer, although a police officer, is independent of the investigation, and has a duty to review the circumstance of the arrest, decide on the necessity of detention and safeguard the suspect's rights and welfare while detained. Any child suspected of committing an offence may be lawfully detained for 24 hours. After 24 hours a superintendent may authorise a further 12 hours detention depending on the circumstances of the case and the child. In order to extend detention any further the police must apply to the magistrates court. The court may allow a further detention up to a maximum of 96 hours without charge (section 42(1) the Police and Criminal Evidence Act 1984, Code of Practice C: 15.2A).

Section 38 PACE provides that when a young person is charged with an offence the custody officer must order their release from police detention with or without bail unless one of the following grounds applies:

(a) the young person's name or address cannot be ascertained, or the custody officer has serious grounds for doubting the truth of a name or address provided;

(b) the custody officer has reasonable grounds for believing that the young person will fail to appear in court;

(c) the custody officer has reasonable grounds for believing that the detention of the young person is necessary to prevent him committing an offence;

(d) where a young person is aged 14 years and above and the custody officer has reasonable grounds for believing that detention is necessary to enable a sample to be taken;

(e) the custody officer has reasonable grounds for believing that detention is necessary to prevent the young person from causing physical injury to another person or from causing loss of or damage to property;

(f) the custody officer has reasonable grounds for believing that detention is necessary to prevent the young person from interfering with the administration of justice or with the investigation of the offence;

(g) the custody officer has reasonable grounds for believing that detention is necessary for the young person's own protection;

(h) there are reasonable grounds for believing that the young person should be detained in the interests of their welfare.

One of the common requirements attached to bail is that of providing one or more sureties. A surety is a person who undertakes to pay the court a specified sum of money in the event of the defendant failing to surrender to custody. If the defendant absconds the surety may be ordered to pay part or all of the sum in which they stood surety. By section 37 Bail Act 1976, where the accused is a young person and his parent stands surety, the court may require that surety to ensure that the young person complies with any conditions of bail; thus the court can require the parent to be a surety for good behaviour.

Where a young person is charged with an offence and the custody officer authorises their continued detention, the custody officer must try to make arrangements for the young person to be taken into the care of the local authority to be detained pending an appearance in court. This requirement does not apply if the custody officer certifies that it is impractical to do so or if no secure accommodation is available and there is a risk to the public of serious harm from the young person. Neither the young person's behaviour, nor the nature of the offence with which they are charged provide grounds for the custody officer to decide that it is impractical to seek to arrange a transfer to the care of the local authority. Similarly, the lack of secure local authority accommodation does not make it impracticable to transfer the young person. A young person must not be placed in a police cell, unless no other secure accommodation is available and the custody officer considers supervising the young person would not be practicable unless they are placed in a cell, or the custody officer considers that a cell provides more comfortable accommodation than other secure accommodation in the police station.

## Restorative justice

The police have essentially four options to choose from after arresting a young person for committing an offence: taking no action; reprimands; final warnings; and invoking the court process. The decision about which course of action to take will be made at the police station by the custody officer who will consider the seriousness of the offence and any police intervention in the past (NACRO, 2000a). A reprimand is intended for a first offence and the final warning is reserved for a second offence. A final warning may be given to those who have committed a first offence which is so serious that a reprimand is not appropriate, but not so serious that a charge must result. A second reprimand is not permissible. Section 56 of the Criminal Justice and Court Services Act 2000 states that the reprimand or final warning does not have to be administered at a police station. Once a final warning is given, any subsequent offending will be dealt with by the youth court, unless the subsequent offending is not considered serious and occurred more than two years after the initial warning was given (section 65(3)(b) Crime and Disorder Act 1998). The statutory scheme thus creates a clear presumption in favour of prosecuting a young offender who has previously been repri-manded and warned. If the young person does not make an admission of guilt, they cannot be reprimanded. The police will decide whether to take no further action or to charge the young person and refer them to the youth court. The police may also seek advice from the Crown Prosecution Service who can decide whether to continue the prosecution.

Section 65 of the Crime and Disorder Act 1998 does not state any criteria by which to determine whether a reprimand or final warning is appropriate, except that the officer concerned must be satisfied that 'it would not be in the public interest for the offender to be prosecuted' (section 65(1)(e) Crime and Disorder Act 1998). Statutory guidance emphasises the central importance of determining the seriousness of the offence (Home Office and Youth Justice Board, 2002). To assist in achieving a consistent approach to assessment, the *Guidance* specifies the use of the Association of Chief Police Officers Gravity Factor System under which all offences can be scored between one, for the most minor offences, and four, for the most serious offending where the young person will always be charged rather than warned. The Scheme specifies that where an offence has a gravity factor of three the police should normally issue a final warning for a first offence, but if the offender does not qualify for a warning they must be charged. The initial gravity scoring for the offence can be upgraded or downgraded by one point in the light of specified aggravating and mitigating factors that can make an offence more or less serious. When assessing the seriousness of an offence the police officer has the option to ask the youth offending team to undertake a prior assessment of the young offender to inform their decision-making. The Scheme has been supplemented by Home Office Circular 2006 which states that in instances where there is doubt about whether to charge 'it will often be useful to seek the opinion of the Crown Prosecution Service at an early stage' (Home Office, 2006).

Avon and Somerset police, and seven other police forces across England and Wales, have been using the Youth Restorative Disposal since April 2008 as a way of addressing the offending behaviour of young people committing minor offences. A police officer trained to use the Youth Restorative Disposal will act on the spot at the time of commission of the offence and oversee a meeting between the offender and the victim to resolve the situation. The aim is to prevent young people being drawn into the criminal justice system.

## Youth Conditional Cautions

Section 48 and Schedule 9 of the Criminal Justice and Immigration Act 2008 extends conditional cautions to children and young persons (by amending the Crime and Disorder Act 1998) as a means of dealing with offenders as an alternative to prosecution. Youth Conditional Cautions, available only for 16 and 17 year olds, provide an additional alternative option at the pre-court stage. They will be used where the offender has either committed an offence which is not suitable to be dealt with by way of reprimand or final warning, or where the offender has already received a reprimand and final warning. Such cases would currently most likely be referred to court, however the Youth Conditional Caution allows a relevant prosecutor, the CPS, to offer a caution with condition(s) attached for certain offences. The decision to administer a Youth Conditional Caution has the effect of suspending any criminal proceedings while the youth is given an opportunity to comply with the agreed conditions. Where the conditions are complied with, a prosecution is not commenced. If an offender fails without reasonable cause to comply with the conditions attached to a conditional caution, the amended Crime and Disorder Act 1998 provides for criminal proceedings in respect of the original offence to be instituted and the caution cancelled.

Youth Conditional Cautions are an out-of-court disposal aimed at reducing the number of young offenders taken to court, where appropriate conditions can meet the justice of the case, taking into account the views of the victim and the behavioural needs of the youth. The cautions provide an opportunity to achieve an early positive response to offending behaviour for those young people willing to admit their offending and to comply with certain conditions. It will operate as the 'next tier' from the reprimand or final warning as a more serious disposal. Once a prosecutor has determined that a Youth Conditional Caution is appropriate in a case, an authorised person will administer the caution. An authorised person includes a police constable, an investigating officer or a person authorised by the CPS. The Youth Conditional Caution may be administered in a police station, court building, YOT premises, the offices of any prosecutor, or any other suitable location consistent with achieving the appropriate impact on the youth.

The role of the police in England and Wales in responding to youth offending can be contrasted with that of the police in other jurisdictions. The next section will examine the role of the police in diverting young offenders from the criminal justice system in the Republic of Ireland and Germany.

## Police power to divert young offenders in other jurisdictions

The main legislation covering youth offending in the Republic of Ireland is the Children Act 2001. One of the important principles of the 2001 Act is that where a child accepts responsibility for their offending behaviour they should be diverted from criminal proceedings, where appropriate. In the Republic of Ireland, if a child becomes involved in offending behaviour and is taken to a police station (known as a Garda station) a Juvenile Liaison Officer (JLO) will deal specifically with the situation. The JLO will explain to the child what is happening and will contact the parent or guardian as soon as possible. The police (known as the Gardaí) may decide to caution the child and refer the child to the Garda Juvenile Diversion Programme. The Garda Juvenile Diversion Programme consists of local community-based activities which work with children. These projects aim to help children move away from behaving in a way that might get them or their friends into trouble with the law. They can help children develop their sense of community and their social skills through different activities. The projects offer opportunities for education, employment training, sport, art, music and other activities. Most projects operate outside of school hours. However, in areas with a high proportion of early school-leavers, activities may also be planned during the daytime. The projects seek to encourage a better quality of life for everyone in the community and to support good relations between the Gardaí and the community. A child may also agree, as part of a caution, a number of actions which they will do to address the hurt that they have caused. This can include an apology to the victim, a form of compensation, a curfew or to take part in a sporting or recreational activity. Supervision of the child in the community for a period of 12 months will usually follow a caution. As part of the community supervision, the Juvenile Liaison Officer may convene a conference bringing together the child, the child's family and any other relevant parties to identify the reasons for the child's behaviour and develop an action plan for preventing any future offending. Thus in the Republic of Ireland the police are under a statutory obligation to caution and supervise young offenders rather than charging them and referring them to court.

Similarly in Germany, the youth justice system will only resort to penal action when absolutely necessary. However, unlike in England and Wales and in the Republic of Ireland, police diversion in the form of 'cautioning' or 'reprimanding' is not allowed in Germany for historical reasons, namely the abuse of police power during the Nazi period. Therefore in Germany the police must refer all criminal offending to the juvenile court. The juvenile court can discharge the case with no further action if social or educational interventions have taken place or if the young person has made efforts to participate in victim–offender reconciliation. Although the role of police diversion does not exist in Germany, nonetheless most young offenders in Germany will be subject to educational measures rather than penal measures.

## Youth court

The youth court is a magistrates court specially constituted to deal with matters concerning 10–18 year old offenders. The youth court is less formal than a magistrates court and operates its own special procedures. Cases are not normally open to the public and there are restrictions on press reporting, but these can be dispensed with if it is in the public interest to do so. Although the youth court will usually sit in the same building as the adult court, a separate room with a separate entrance and exit from the adult court will be used. The youth court panel will consist of three experienced magistrates who have had at least two years experience of working in the adult criminal courts. The panel will usually contain male and female members. Youth court magistrates will have undergone specific training including youth court observations, training on the relevant law and sentencing procedures, and visits to young offender institutions. The youth court panel may be members of the lay judiciary, that is members of the community who have volunteered to become magistrates and who are not legally qualified. As local volunteers they will have knowledge of the local community and the services which are available. Magistrates will usually sit as a panel of three. A justices' clerk will provide them with legal advice on their powers, the law, sentencing and evidence. Alternatively the youth court may be presided over by a District judge, who is a lawyer appointed to sit as a full-time magistrate. They usually sit alone.

The youth court sits at the lowest level of the court structure in England and Wales. The youth court has the power to sentence children aged 12–17 years to Detention and Training Orders for up to 24 months, as well as to a range of community sentences. Youth courts seek to fully engage with the children appearing in court and with their families. Magistrates are trained to engage directly with the child and ensure, so far as is possible and reasonable, that they are able to participate fully in the proceedings. The court is, where possible, arranged so that all involved are on the same level and the child is able to sit with or near their parents (or guardians) and legal representative. Members of the public are not allowed to observe the court hearings. The victim(s) of the crime can attend the hearings of the court, which is required to consider the needs and wishes of victims.

Section 49 of the Children and Young Persons Act 1933 restricts the reporting of proceedings in the youth court and prohibits the publication of any report or picture which might reveal, or lead to the revealing of, the name, address or school of young persons concerned in the proceedings. This prohibition is subject to certain exceptions where it is in the public interest to do so. The court must afford an opportunity for representations to be made before making an order to dispense with the restriction on reporting. The joint Lord Chancellors Department and Home Office guidance encourages the court to consider lifting restrictions in cases where the nature of the young person's offending is persistent or serious or has impacted on a number of people in the local community, or where alerting others to the young person's behaviour would help prevent further offending (Lord Chancellor's Department *et al.*, 1999).

The youth court is guided by a number of important statutory principles. The first is enshrined in section 37 of the Crime and Disorder Act 1998 and provides that it shall be the principal aim of the youth justice system to prevent offending by children and young persons. Section 44 of the Children and Young Persons Act 1933 requires that the child's welfare shall be the paramount concern of the court. The Criminal Justice Act 1991 established the principle of proportionality, which means that the sentence of the court should fit the seriousness of the crime. Under section 153 of the Criminal Justice Act 2003 a custodial sentence must be for the shortest term commensurate with the seriousness of the offence or offences.

The youth court can use Pre-Sentence Reports (PSR) when sentencing young people to custody. The Criminal Justice Act 2003 defines the PSR as a written report produced, where the defendant is under 18 years of age, by a probation officer, social worker or member of a YOT with a view to assisting the court in determining the most suitable method of dealing with an offender (section 158 Criminal Justice Act 2003). There is a statutory presumption in favour of the court obtaining and considering a PSR before it imposes a custodial sentence. The PSR will usually provide an analysis of the factors that are relevant to the young person's criminal behaviour, and an independent assessment of the seriousness of the current offending. Also included in the PSR will be an account of the young person's personal circumstances to the extent that they contribute to an understanding of the offending behaviour. PSRs will usually provide an assessment of the risk of reoffending, and any resulting harm, framed in the context of what forms of intervention may reduce the risk. Also included will be a description of a programme of intervention which is commensurate with the seriousness of the offence, addresses the young person's welfare needs and other factors highlighted in the offence analysis; and serves to reduce risk. The PSR will usually conclude with a single proposal that matches the needs of the young persons to the most suitable form of disposal within the range of penalties proportionate to the offending (NACRO, 2003).

The police are at the forefront of detecting and responding to youth offending. Accordingly the police have the power to stop, search, arrest, question and detain any young person suspected of involvement in offending behaviour. However, suspected young people also have rights which the police must protect, such as the right to have an appropriate adult present at any questioning and the right to consult with a solicitor. The police have several options available to them in terms of how they respond to a young person who has admitted offending. They can take no further action, issue a reprimand, final warning or a Youth Conditional Caution. If the young person does not admit responsibility for offending, the police can take no further action or charge the young person and refer them to the youth court for trial and sentencing. A young person may also be referred to the youth court for trial where they have offended previously or they have engaged in serious offending. The youth court is specially designed to take account of the unique needs and vulnerabilities of young people. The youth court must decide, based on the evidence, whether the young person is guilty or not. If the young person is found to be guilty, the youth court has a number of sentencing options; these options will be examined in detail in Chapters 9, 10 and 11. If the case involves very serious offending, the youth court will send the case to the Crown Court for trial and sentencing. Cases referred to the Crown Court will be examined in Chapter 12.

---

**Discussion topic**

Outline the main differences between the youth court and adult court.

---

*Comment*

The youth court has a more informal setting than an adult court as it aims to engage with young people and help them to understand the court process. Some of the significant differences between youth courts and adult courts include the following:

- The general public are excluded from youth courts.
- In the youth court the bench of magistrates hearing the case must consist of no more than three magistrates and must include a man and a woman.
- If a young person is under 16 years of age, their parents/guardian must attend the youth court.
- Where a young person is not legally represented the court may permit his parent or guardian to assist in conducting his defence.
- The media may not report the name or any other identifying details of the young person charged. Journalists are allowed to be present at the youth court to report on the case but they cannot identify the young person.

## Suggested further reading

Brookman, F. and Pierpoint, H. (2003) 'Access to legal aid for young suspects', *Howard Journal of Criminal Justice*, 42, 5, 452–70.

Moore, S. (2000) 'Child incarceration and the new youth justice' in Goldson, B. (ed.) *The New Youth Justice*, Dorset: Russell House, pp. 115–28.

Pierpoint, H. (2006) 'Reconstructing the role of the appropriate adult in England and Wales', *Criminology and Criminal Justice*, 6, 2, 219–37.

# 9 Restorative justice in the English youth justice system

## Introduction

Restorative justice is about repairing the harm caused by anti-social and criminal behaviour. The inclusion of the victim is generally seen as an important feature of restorative justice. Restorative justice processes aim to hold offenders accountable by requiring them to explain how they think their actions may have affected others. It is hoped that this process will also help the victim. Restorative justice is not concerned with fact finding but with finding an appropriate response to an admitted offence. This chapter will examine the origins and role of restorative justice in the English youth justice system.

The United Nations Office of Drugs and Crime (2006: 6) defines restorative justice as a process in which the victim and the offenders, and any other individuals affected by a crime, participate actively in the resolution of matters arising from the crime, usually with the help of a facilitator. Restorative justice allows the response to criminal behaviour to balance the needs of the community, the victims and the offenders. Dignan (1999) summarises the most important aims of the restorative approach as including: engaging with offenders to try to bring home the consequences of their actions and the impact of their behaviour on the victims; encouraging and facilitating the provision of appropriate forms of reparation for the offence; and seeking reconciliation between victim and offender. Restorative justice is heralded as a just and fair way to deal with criminal behaviour as it focusses on the victim and community where the offending occurred and is dealt with by those most affected by it (Richardson, 1997; Morris, 2002).

## Origins of restorative justice

Restorative justice is rooted in ancient processes of conflict resolution founded on holistic and communitarian values, full voluntary participation of all participants, respect for the individual, including the offender and their social environment, and emphasises safety and the healing of harm through expressions of feelings regarding the impact of the crime (Moore and Mitchell, 2009: 33). Early examples of restorative justice can be found in traditional Maori culture in New Zealand. The Maori approach involved communities coming together in a public meeting place to resolve disputes in the presence of the local community and community leaders. Disputes were discussed and a solution reached which promoted community harmony rather than private vengeance. By the early 1980s in New Zealand concern was mounting regarding traditional approaches to youth offending. Maori families became frustrated with the over-representation of their young people in the criminal justice system. They proposed a return to their traditional justice processes which involved offenders, victims and communities. The Children, Young Persons and their Family Act 1989 responded to these concerns by giving statutory form to conferencing procedures to achieve responsible reconciliation. The 1989 New Zealand Act provided that all young people charged with an offence, provided it was not a very serious offence, are automatically referred to a family group conference. The offender, the offender's family, the victim and the victim's family are invited to attend. These parties are then required to negotiate an agreement regarding an appropriate resolution of the offending incident. The agreement will usually involve an apology or community work. Once the parties have made an agreement a Youth Justice Coordinator liaises with the youth court and the police. The role of the coordinator is to ensure that any agreement is not unduly severe or indeterminate and that there is equality of treatment with similar offences. If no agreement is reached, then the youth court imposes a solution. The coordinator will ensure that the offender is not marginalised from the community, but accepted as a key participant in the decision-making. In New Zealand the family group conference is used not only for lesser crimes, but also for offences involving burglary, arson and rape.

Under international law, the UK is required to develop such restorative justice processes as part of the youth justice system. Article 40(3) of the United Nations Convention on the Rights of the Child requires state parties to develop measures for dealing with young offenders without resorting to judicial proceedings, provided that human rights are respected. The United Nations Committee on the Rights of the Child believes that diversion avoids stigmatising the child and is cost effective (United Nations Committee on the Rights of the Child, 2007: 11).

## Restorative justice in the English youth justice system

By 1997 New Labour wanted to incorporate these restorative principles and practices into the new youth justice system in order to create a victim-centred system while also encouraging offenders to take responsibility for their actions and prevent future offending (Home Office, 1997a). New Labour saw restorative justice principles as a vehicle for achieving its pledge to be 'tough on crime, tough on the causes of crime'. The White Paper *No*

*More Excuses* defines restorative justice as including 'restoration, reintegration and responsibility' and furthermore defines these terms. Restoration is characterised as young offenders apologising to their victims and making amends for the harm they have done. Reintegration involves young offenders paying their debt to society, putting their crimes behind them and rejoining the law-abiding community. Responsibility involves young offenders and their parents facing the consequences of their offending behaviour and taking responsibility for preventing further offending (Home Office, 1997a: 9.21)

The main thrust of restorative justice in the English youth justice system is to promote more effective ways of preventing offending by young people by undertaking early interventions that seek to address the known causes of their anti-social and offending behaviour. These efforts aim to make young people accountable for what they have done by requiring them to undertake some reparation to the victim and/or the community. Statutory Guidance outlines the forms of reparation that are considered appropriate as including letters of apology, restorative conferences, and practical reparative activity related to the offence (Home Office, 2000: 55). In England and Wales restorative justice has been equated with victim–offender mediation. Victim–offender mediation is a voluntary process of communication between a victim of crime and the offender who committed the crime. It can be direct, where parties meet face to face, or indirect, where information is exchanged between the parties. In either case, the process is managed by a mediator who acts as a communication channel between the two parties. Mediators are neutral and do not represent either side. This process offers victims a chance to speak about how they have been affected by what has happened, to say what might repair the harm done to them, and to ask questions and get answers from the one person who can answer them, namely the offender. For offenders, it offers the opportunity to take responsibility for what they have done, to apologise for the harm they have caused and to make amends. Reparation is part of the pre-trial stage and the post conviction stage in the English youth justice system.

## Restorative justice at the pre-trial stage

Section 65 of the Crime and Disorder Act 1998 provides that a police officer can respond to a young person's first offence with a final warning depending on its seriousness. The final warning should be delivered by a police officer in the presence of parents or a responsible adult. A final warning may only be given if the police are satisfied that it would not be in the public interest to prosecute. The young offender must make a clear and reliable admission to all elements of the offence and have not previously been convicted in court. There must also be evidence against the young person sufficient to give a realistic prospect of conviction if the young person were prosecuted. When a final warning is administered, the police officer is required to refer the young person to the local youth offending team for 'assessment' for suitability for an intervention programme (section 66 Crime and Disorder Act 1998). The youth offending team (YOT) comprises representatives from the police, probation, education and health authorities and the local authority. The YOT has primary responsibility for providing a multi-agency service for children and young people who are involved in offending behaviour and working with young offenders in order to prevent further offending (section 41 Crime and Disorder Act 1998).

Suitability for an intervention programme is assessed by ASSET. ASSET is the assessment profile that the Youth Justice Board has developed with the Centre for Criminological Research at Oxford University for use with all young people who enter and leave the youth justice system. ASSET allows YOTs to assess the needs of young people and to match these needs with appropriate intervention programmes. ASSET provides a structured, comprehensive and consistent means of assessing the needs of young people and the risk of their reoffending or causing harm to themselves or others. The profile covers all areas of the young person's life linked to their offending behaviour, including living arrangements, family and personal relationships, education, employment and training, lifestyle, substance abuse, physical health, emotional and mental health and cognitive and behavioural development. The main function of ASSET is to identify needs before interventions are planned and implemented (Audit Commission, 2004). ASSET allows for the development of an intervention programme to address the particular needs of the individual offender.

If the 'assessment' indicates the need for assistance, and the presumption is that it will (Home Office, 1997a) the youth offending team will draw up a detailed rehabilitation programme whose over-riding objective will be to prevent reoffending by addressing the causes of the young person's offending behaviour (Home Office, 2000). As seen in Chapter 7, YOTs have taken the lead in creating schemes to provide purposeful and engaging activities to young people who have offended or are at risk of offending. Examples of such schemes include Youth Inclusion Programmes (YIPs), Positive Activities for Young People, mentoring programmes and parenting programmes. Youth offending teams are thus offering a large selection of youth crime prevention programmes which aim to tackle juvenile offending behaviour at the different stages of its development.

Reprimands and final warnings remain on the Police National Computer for a period of five years and are both cited in court hearings if a young person engages in subsequent offending. Compliance and non-compliance with a final warning programme is cited in YOT court reports (Evans and Puech, 2001). Thus a young person's engagement with a final warning programme can have a potentially detrimental effect on future sentencing options for the young person.

## Restorative justice disposals available to the youth court

The Youth Justice and Criminal Evidence Act 1999 introduced the referral order as a new primary sentencing disposal for 10–17 year olds pleading guilty and convicted for the first time. The disposal involves referring the young offender to a youth offender panel (YOP). The youth offender panel includes lay members from the community and one member of a local youth offending team. The YOP provides a forum where the young offender, members of his family and, if appropriate, the victim can consider the circumstances surrounding the offence and the effect on the victim. The youth offender panel then establishes a 'programme of behaviour' with the young offender to address his offending behaviour which the child will be obliged to observe. The programme of behaviour can include: financial or other reparation to the victim; mediation with the victim; unpaid work or service in the community; attendance at school, educational establishment or work; participation in specified activities such as alcohol or drug treatment, counselling, courses addressing offending behaviour; or education or training. The principal aim of the programme of behaviour is the prevention of reoffending by the child (section 8 Crime and Disorder Act 1998). Part III of the Powers of Criminal Courts (Sentencing) Act 2000 provides that the referral order is to become the standard sentence imposed by the youth courts, or other magistrates court, for all first time offenders under the age of 18 years unless their offending is so serious that it warrants custody or the court orders an absolute discharge or makes a hospital order.

An 18 month evaluation of referral orders in 11 pilot areas in England and Wales in 2001 found that most youth offender panels had established themselves as deliberative and participatory forums in which the central parties felt able to participate (Newburn *et al.*, 2002). This evaluation examined the implementation processes and the impact of referral orders on the agencies and individuals involved and on sentencing and reoffending between March 2001 and August 2001. Furthermore, the research found that in 70 per cent of observed panels, young offenders acknowledged full responsibility for their offending. Most of the young people interviewed, and their parents, were positive about the experience of the referral order; they believed that it gave them a chance to speak for themselves, and to think about their actions and the impact of their offending on others. In fact young people completed the contract successfully in 74 per cent of cases where a panel met. The victims' experience of the panel meetings was also overwhelmingly positive. Most victims (70 per cent) felt that the panel had taken account of what they had said when deciding what should be done. By the end of the panel meeting the majority of victims (69 per cent) felt that the offender had a proper understanding of the harm that had been caused.

## Problems with the restorative justice approach

It is evident that a considerable range of initiatives intended to discourage juvenile anti-social and offending behaviour have been introduced, together with a growing understanding of the parameters and requirements of appropriate provision to meet the individual and diverse needs of young people who engage in anti-social and offending behaviour. However in England and Wales the restorative elements are peripheral to the work of the youth justice system. They are additions rather than defining components of a youth justice system that is committed to punishment and incarceration. In Scotland and New Zealand, where the children's hearing system and family group conference have both succeeded, the restorative justice arrangements were substitutes for court appearances and not additions to the system. The Youth Justice Board and YOTs in England and Wales are required to manage custodial sentences of young offenders along with many other tasks related to court convictions. These other roles have placed constraints on the capacity of YOTs to deliver restorative justice to victims, especially in first offender cases receiving reprimands and final warnings.

The rule of law requires that people are treated fairly in relation to one another. Restorative justice may encourage inconsistency in dealing with similar cases and lacks the transparency of the criminal justice system. Ashworth argues that the response to offending behaviour should be decided by reference to publicly debated and democratically determined policies that show respect for the human rights of victims and offenders (Ashworth, 2003). A characteristic of restorative justice is that it draws into the criminal justice system both the victim and the wider community. A consequence of this may be that the rule of law is sacrificed. If different communities and victims have different standards the result may be a form of 'justice by geography' or 'postcode lottery'. Two people from a similar background committing a similar offence but in different localities may receive different responses. This violates the rule of law which requires justice to be administered consistently so that individuals do not find themselves subject to variable standards in different courts.

The rights of the victim may be allowed to assume greater importance than those of a damaged offender. Punishment should be proportionate to the offence committed and similar offences and offenders should result in similar sentences. The involvement of victims undermines this as the views of victims may vary, some may be forgiving and others may be vindictive. If victim satisfaction is an aim of restorative justice, then proportionate sentencing is unlikely to form part of this.

Article 6 of the European Convention on Human Rights provides that everyone has a right to a fair trial hearing by an independent and impartial tribunal. The victim is not impartial, thus Article 6 may be violated. Also Braithwaite questions the role of the police in facilitating a conference (Braithwaite, 1999). Does this make the police investigator, prosecutor, judge and jury? The decision to administer a reprimand or final warning rests with the police, who may adopt a variable attitude to this.

Within restorative programmes the burden tends to remain on individuals to atone or change their behaviour, rather than on the state to recognise that it also has a responsibility (within international conventions and rules) to its citizens (Haines and O'Mahony, 2006). For example Article 6 of the European Convention on Human Rights provides for the right to a fair trial with legal representation and a right to appeal. The introduction of lay youth offender panels deliberating on 'programmes of behaviour' with no legal representation would appear to be in denial of such rights (Goldson, 2000b). More seriously, many of the principles of restorative justice which rely on informality, flexibility and discretion sit uneasily against legal requirements for due process and a fair and just trial. This issue was considered in the case of *R (on the application of U.) v Commissioner of Police for the Metropolitan and R (on the application of R.) v Durham Constabulary* ([2003] Crim LR 349) which concerned two 15-year-old boys who had admitted indecently assaulting young girls. In both cases the police determined that they boys would receive a final warning. The boys were then required to register under the provisions of the Sex Offender Act 1997. The Crime and Disorder Act 1998 extended the registration requirements to those reprimanded or warned under the provisions of the 1998 Act. Neither boy had been made aware during their dealings with the police that such registration would be a consequence of accepting the final warning. Both boys asserted that they would not have accepted the final warning had they been aware of this consequence, instead they would have preferred to have the allegations against them tried in court. The court held that the boys had been entitled to a fair trial of the allegations against them, but instead were subjected to an administrative process that had the effect of publicly pronouncing their guilt by being recorded in the Police National Computer. Latham LJ did not condemn the system of reprimands and final warnings as being in breach of Article 6 of the European Convention on Human Rights. But the court held that these procedures must involve an informed consent to the procedure being adopted. The court held that the appropriate practice must be to ensure that the offender, his parent, carer or any other appropriate adult, are all told of the consequences of the warning prior to it being given and asked whether they consent to the suggested course of action. Similarly the United Nations Committee on the Rights of the Child recommend that such processes should only be used where the young person acknowledges their responsibility, freely gives their consent to the restorative justice process and where such acknowledgement of responsibility will not be used against them in subsequent legal proceedings (United Nations Committee on the Rights of the Child, 2007: 13).

The compulsory nature of reparation may undermine the benefits to the offender. The compulsory nature risks reparation becoming routine rather than meaningful (Williams, 2001). The coercive penal context offends traditional restorative ideals of voluntariness (Crawford and Newburn, 2003: 238). YOTs and YOPs have the power to produce programmes for young offenders that are far more intrusive and punitive than may be merited, thereby infringing the proportionality principle. A danger also remains that any form of compulsory restoration may degenerate into a ceremony of public shaming and degradation, particularly when it operates within a system of justice whose primary intent is no longer the protection of the child's welfare.

Victims have a right to justice, and a right not to be further damaged by the processes of dealing with the offence. Their right to justice includes the expectation that offenders will be appropriately dealt with and the wrongness of their actions condemned. Participation in mediation may help victims to achieve this even more surely than if the case is left to normal justice processes, and it may also serve their other interests, of which a court takes little cognisance. Nevertheless, there is also the possibility of this not happening, and they may feel aggrieved at the outcome.

Reprimands and final warnings mean that if a young person comes to the attention of the police on two occasions, depending on the seriousness of the offence, then a third time will result in a court appearance regardless of the seriousness of the offence. This rigid approach risks undermining efforts to divert large numbers of young people from the youth justice system and risks prematurely launching children into the criminal justice system. *R v Durham Constabulary and another ex parte R (FC)* ([2005] UKHL 21) involved a 15-year-old youth who had received a final warning for indecent assault. Lady Hale, in the House of Lords, acknowledged the lack of flexibility in reprimands and final warnings and felt that this was inconsistent with the objective of diverting children from the criminal justice system and that it seriously risks offending against the principle that intervention must be proportionate both to the circumstances of the offence and the offender. If young people are diverted from the youth justice system they have the potential to avoid a criminal record and an opportunity to reintegrate into society. The rigid nature of the system of reprimands and final warnings have the potential to snare young people who would not have been embroiled in the youth justice system if these measures were not in place (Fox *et al.*, 2006). Thus it is important that restorative justice processes are used as an alternative criminal justice response, rather than an additional one.

The final warning is a sanction which combines notions of deterrence, via formal procedures that make clear the consequences of further criminal activity, and reform, from the inclusion of a requirement for referral to the YOT for assessment and a 'change' programme (Hine, 2007). The final warning ignores the possible benefits of a further warning. This inflexibility has ensured that the police have lost their discretion to deal with cases informally and has resulted in the youth court being inundated with petty cases.

Young people, as young as 10 years of age and without legal representation, may feel forced into agreeing plans. As there is no person involved who is responsible for protecting the child's welfare, welfare concerns may become marginalised. An offender may be encouraged to admit guilt without legal advice merely to stay out of court. Any final warning given may then be cited in court in subsequent criminal proceedings. Moreover, any young offender in court charged with an offence within two years of receiving a final warning or reprimand is unable to be given a conditional discharge, unless the circumstances are exceptional. Instead the young person will receive a penalty, probably a referral order, thus progressing further down the road to a serious criminal conviction. This order may be made in relation to trivial offences, thus infringing the concept of proportionality. Furthermore, restoration assumes offenders are fully rational decision makers, yet in most other spheres children are assumed to have a limited capacity.

*Table 9.1*  Use of restorative justice in the English youth justice system

| | |
|---|---|
| Pre-crime | YISPs (Youth Inclusion and Support Panels) |
| | Anti Social Behaviour Contracts |
| | On Track |
| | Sure Start |
| | PAYP (Positive Activities for Young People) |
| Pre-trial | Youth Restorative Disposal |
| | Reprimand |
| | Final Warning |
| Trial | Referral Order |

Restorative justice processes create the opportunity for the offender, and the offender's family, to face the consequences of their behaviour and reintegrate them into the community, while also allowing the victim a role in deciding how to respond to the young person's behaviour. However in the English youth justice system, restorative processes sit alongside punitive orders such as ASBOs, parenting orders and detention and training orders. The restorative justice processes have lowered the threshold at which young people are drawn into the youth justice system in England and Wales, which has resulted in greater numbers of young people being processed by the police and the courts and rising numbers of young people in custody.

---

### Discussion topic

How does restorative justice compare with traditional justice in preventing youth crime?

---

## Comment

Restorative justice is based on the principle of involving all those affected by a crime, including the victim, the offender and the offender's family. Restorative justice processes involve adopting a problem-solving approach to dealing with the aftermath of an offence. The primary aims of restorative processes are to attend to the needs of the victim, prevent further offending by reintegrating the offender into the community, enable the offender to assume responsibility for their actions and to avoid involvement in the criminal justice system (Marshall, 1999: 9). Traditional criminal justice procedures are not particularly concerned with the needs of the victim and only limited action is taken to reintegrate the offender into the community. Offenders are only required to suffer punishment for their behaviour, rather than being provided with the opportunity to make good what they have done. Criminal justice procedures do not involve the wider community.

## Suggested further reading

Crawford, A. and Newburn, T. (2003) *Youth Offending and Restorative Justice*, Cullompton: Willan.

Gelsthorpe, L. and Morris, A. (2002) 'Restorative youth justice: the last vestiges of welfare?', in Muncie, J., Hughes, G. and McLaughlin, E. *Youth Justice Critical Readings*, London: Sage, pp. 238–54.

Newbury, A. (2008) 'Youth Crime: Whose Responsibility?' *Journal of Law and Society*, 35, 1, 131–49.

# 10 Sentencing options available to the youth court

## Introduction

You have already seen in Chapter 9 that the standard sentence for most first time offenders convicted in the youth court will be a referral order. This chapter will examine the other sentencing options available to the youth court for young people who do not qualify for a referral order, namely community sentences and custody.

## Community sentences

There are a range of community sentences available to the youth court, including the supervision order, action plan order, reparation order, attendance centre order, community rehabilitation order, the community punishment order and youth rehabilitation orders.

### Supervision order

Although the Children Act 1989 removed from the youth court the power to order a young person into the care of a local authority, it is still possible for a young offender whose home circumstances are thought to contribute to offending to be placed in local authority accommodation. A supervision order can be made in relation to an offender aged between 10 and 17 years old and found guilty of any offence other than an offence of murder (section 7(7)(b) Children and Young Persons Act 1969). The effect of the supervision order is to place the young offender under the supervision of a local authority, probation officer or member of the youth offending team, whose duty is to 'advise, assist and befriend the supervised person' (sections 63–68, Powers of Criminal Courts (Sentencing) Act 2000). Programmes designed to address the offending behaviour will be undertaken, for example the supervision order may require the young person to remain for specified periods at a specified place, to refrain from participating in specified activities, to submit to medical or psychiatric treatment, to make reparation provided the victim consents to this (section 71, Crime and Disorder Act

1998), or require the young offender to live in local authority accommoda-tion (known as a 'residence requirement'). The requirement to reside in local authority accommodation was introduced by the Children Act 1989 to replace the courts' previous power to make a care order in criminal proceed-ings. The intention was to retain some provision for removing a child from home for a limited period in order to provide an opportunity for both the young person and their family to address any specific issues which are causing the young person to engage in offending. The supervision order is designed to cater for a complexity of criminogenic needs and to provide a response for high tariff offending. In general, the supervision order is appro-priate 'when an ... extended period of supervision is required because of the frequency or seriousness of the offending. It should ... tackle the full range of offender needs associated with offending' (Youth Justice Board, 2002b).

### Other community sentences

The youth court previously had the option of making an action plan order (section 69, Powers of Criminal Courts (Sentencing) Act 2000), a reparation order (sections 73–75, Powers of Criminal Courts (Sentencing) Act 2000) or an attendance centre order (section 60, Powers of Criminal Courts (Sentencing) Act 2000) if the court considered that to do so would prevent reoffending or rehabilitate the offender. These orders required the offender, respectively: to comply with a three month action plan supervised by a probation officer, a social worker or a member of a youth offending team; to make specified reparation to the victim of the offending or to the community; or to attend a local centre for a maximum of three hours per day to receive instruction on social skills and physical training. The primary intention of the attendance centre order was to restrict the young person's leisure time. Attendance centres run programmes to provide young people with basic life skills such as literacy and numeracy, cookery, first aid and financial management, as well as victim awareness sessions, drugs and alcohol awareness and sexual health matters. The community rehabilitation order and the community punishment order are only available for convicted 16 and 17 year olds. The community rehabilitation order is similar to the supervision order, whereas the community punishment order requires the young person to do unpaid community work which is supervised by the Probation Service.

### Youth rehabilitation order

The Criminal Justice and Immigration Act 2008 provides for youth rehabili-tation orders which forms a new community sentence for persons under 18 years. The youth rehabilitation order (YRO) will be the standard commu-nity sentence for the majority of young offenders and abolishes all of the previous community orders. The YRO empowers a court to choose from a menu of different requirements with which an offender must comply with. A YRO may include the following:

- an activity requirement;
- a supervision requirement;
- if aged 16 or 17 years, an unpaid work requirement;
- a programme requirement;
- an attendance centre requirement;
- a prohibited activity requirement;
- a curfew requirement;
- an exclusion requirement;
- a residence requirement;
- a local authority residence requirement;
- a mental health requirement;
- a drug treatment requirement;
- a drug testing requirement;
- an intoxicating substance treatment requirement;
- an electronic monitoring requirement.

The 2008 Act thus provides for a single youth rehabilitation order within which a court may include one or more requirements variously designed to provide for punishment, protection of the public, reducing reoffending and reparation. The requirement chosen by the court must be the most suitable for the offender and the restriction of liberty must be commensurate with the seriousness of the offence (section 148 Criminal Justice and Immigration Act 2008). The court must be satisfied that the offence is 'serious enough' to justify imposition of a youth rehabilitation order (section 148(1) Criminal Justice and Immigration Act 2008). However the court may impose a youth rehabilitation order for an offence that is not imprisonable, but not for an offender who would qualify for a referral order. A youth rehabilitation order with intensive supervision and surveillance or with fostering is also available, but these may only be imposed where a custodial sentence would otherwise have been appropriate.

The youth rehabilitation order with intensive supervision and surveillance and the youth rehabilitation order with fostering may be made where the court is dealing with a young person for an offence punishable with custody, and custody would be an appropriate offence. Additionally if the offender was under 15 years of age at the time of commission of the offence, the court needs to be satisfied that the offender is a 'persistent offender'. The intensive supervision and surveillance orders provide for the offender to participate in activities or residential exercises for a maximum of 180 days. A fostering requirement requires the young offender to reside with a local authority foster parent for a period not exceeding 12 months. The court must be satisfied that a significant factor in the young person's offending behaviour was the circumstances in which the young person was living. A fostering requirement cannot be included with an intensive supervision and surveillance order. If the court chooses to impose a custodial sentence the court must state its reasons for being satisfied that the offence is so serious that no other sanction is appropriate and why a youth rehabilitation order with intensive supervision and surveillance or with fostering cannot be justified (section 174(4B) Criminal Justice Act 2003, as amended by schedule 4, 80(3) Criminal Justice and Immigration Act 2008).

The youth rehabilitation order aims to be a more individualised risk and needs-based approach to community sentencing providing courts with a greater choice. Courts will be expected to use the youth rehabilitation order on multiple occasions. The Youth Justice Board's Scaled Approach programme which employs a tiered model for interventions, based on risk, has been designed to support the youth rehabilitation order. The Scaled Approach means that young people who offend will receive interventions that are better tailored to meet their specific needs, according to their risk of reoffending or causing serious harm to others. Interventions will be intentionally differentiated according to the risks of reconviction and the needs of young people. The assessment will be based on ASSET and pre-sentence reports (Youth Justice Board, 2007). The Scaled Approach will be more prescriptive on the level and type of intervention, which will be directly dependent on both the seriousness of the offence, ASSET score and pre-sentence reports – the higher the score, the more intervention there will be (Youth Justice Board, 2007). This potentially creates a problem: if the young person commits a serious offence and is given a community order with minimal intervention because he presents with few assessed risks, how will the credibility of the sentence be viewed? (Sutherland, 2009: 55) Alternatively, if two young people commit the same offence but present with very different risk assessments: the one with the high score will receive more intervention than the one with the low score, even though they have committed the same offence. Accordingly a young person presenting with a list of issues which are beyond their control, such as living in a deprived neighbourhood and having family members who are criminals, may be subject to a greater deprivation of their liberty than one who does not (Sutherland, 2009: 56–7).

Where the youth rehabilitation order has been breached the court has the power to allow the order to continue in its original form, impose a fine, amend the terms of the order, or revoke the order and resentence the offender. If amending the terms of the order, the court can impose any requirement that it could have imposed when making the order in addition to or in substitution of any requirements contained in the order. If an offender has 'wilfully and persistently' failed to comply with the terms of a youth rehabilitation order, the court may make an order with intensive supervision and surveillance, even where the offence is not an imprisonable offence. The court may also impose a four month detention and training

*Table 10.1* Community sentences

| | |
|---|---|
| Children and Young Persons Act 1969 – Power of Criminal Courts (Sentencing) Act 2000 | Supervision order<br>Action plan order<br>Reparation order<br>Attendance centre order<br>Community rehabilitation order<br>Community punishment order |
| Criminal Justice and Immigration Act 2008 | Youth rehabilitation order |

order in these circumstances (schedule 2 Criminal Justice and Immigration Act 2008). Detention and training orders will be discussed later in this chapter.

## Use of custody

England and Wales lock up more young people than any other country in Western Europe. Large numbers of these young people sentenced to custody do not pose a serious risk to the community and, indeed, by leading to broken links with family, friends, education, work and leisure they may become a significantly greater danger upon their release (Goldson and Peters, 2000). For reasons that appear political rather than pragmatic, the example followed is usually the United States of America whose punitive values are so infamous that Simon (2001) refers to an emergent penality of cruelty characterised in the USA by the death penalty for young people (until its eventual abolition in March 2005), boot camps, juvenile court waivers and numerous shame sanctions. This section will examine the history of custody in the English youth justice system and consider the role custody plays in the current youth justice system in England and Wales. It will also assess whether custody helps in preventing reoffending or whether it wastefully diverts considerable resources from community provision to high security institutions.

### History of the use of custody in the youth justice system

You will recall from Chapter 1 that the first penal institution solely for young people in England was opened at Parkhurst in 1838. Parkhurst was designed to segregate young offenders from adult offenders and thus prevent young people from being tainted by adults in prison. This was followed by the development of reformatories and industrial schools in the mid-nineteenth century. Reformatory schools were designed to provide industrial training to young offenders, whereas industrial schools were designed to help vulnerable children before they committed a crime. The beginning of the twentieth century saw the development of a new specialist detention centre for young people – the borstal. The Prevention of Crime Act 1908 allowed for young offenders, between the ages of 16 and 21 years, to be sentenced to a borstal for a period of between one and three years. Borstal training involved a regime of hard physical work, technical and educational instruction, character formation, respect for authority and a strong moral atmosphere. The Children and Young Persons Act 1933 amalgamated industrial schools and reformatories into 'approved schools'. The 1933 Act allowed for offenders and non-offenders to be sent to approved schools for up to 3 years where the regime was aimed at education and discipline, rather than punishment. The Criminal Justice Act 1948 introduced detention centres for those aged between 14 and 17 years, and attendance centres for those aged between 8 and 17 years. Detention centres were designed for young offenders who did not require long term training in an approved school or borstal, but for whom non-custodial measures were inappropriate. Detention centres were abolished in 1988. Attendance centres were intended to punish young people by depriving them of their leisure time and were considered a form of judicial school detention.

In the 1980s borstals were abolished and replaced with youth custody centres. Youth custody centres were replaced by young offender institutions in 1988. The Criminal Justice Act 1991 introduced detention in a young offender institution as a new uniform custodial sentence and raised the minimum age at which custody could be imposed in the youth court from 14 to 15 years. The Criminal Justice and Public Order Act 1994 increased the maximum length of detention in a young offender institution from 12–24 months for 15–17 year olds. The 1994 Act also introduced a new custodial sentence, the secure training order, for those aged between 12 and 14 years. In the UK, the first American-style boot camp opened in 1996 at Thorn Cross Young Offender Institution in Cheshire, employing a 'high intensity' mixture of education, discipline and training. A second camp was opened at the Military Corrective Training Centre in Colchester in 1997 which promised an even more Spartan regime. Due to excessive costs the Colchester camp closed less than one year later.

### The use of custody in the current youth justice system

The Crime and Disorder Act 1998 created the generic custodial sanction of the detention and training order (DTO) (section 73(2)(b)). A DTO can be given to any 15–17 year old for any offence considered serious enough to warrant custody and to 12–14 year olds who are considered persistent offenders. The orders are for between four and fourteen months. Half of the order is served in the community under the supervision of a social worker, probation officer or a member of a YOT, and the other half is served in custody. To use custody, the youth court must be satisfied that the offence is so serious that no other type of penalty can be justified (section 152 Criminal Justice Act 2003), or, in the case of a violent or sexual offence, that only a custodial sentence will be adequate to protect the public from serious harm from the offender (section 79(2) Powers of Criminal Courts (Sentencing) Act 2000). For those aged 12–14 the youth court must also be of the opinion that they are both persistent and dangerous (Power of Criminal Court (Sentencing) Act 2000 section 100(2)(b)), whereas for those aged between 15–17 the court must merely be of the opinion that they are persistent offenders (Power of Criminal Court (Sentencing) Act 2000 section 100(2)(a)).

Persistent is not defined and it is for the court to decide on a case by case basis when repeat offending becomes persistent by 'applying the commonly understood meaning of the term to the facts of the case' (*R v C* (2000) *The Times* 11th October) and using 'the good sense of the court' (*R v DB* [2001] Crim LR 50). In *R v C* the court ruled that the non-statutory definition of persistence provided by the Home Office (1997a), namely that an offender sentenced on three or more separate occasions and arrested again within three years of the last sentencing occasion, was irrelevant in determining persistence for the purposes of a DTO. The non-statutory definition was developed for the purposes of fast-tracking 'persistent' offenders through the youth justice system. In determining persistence the court is entitled to have regard to any offence which gave rise to a reprimand or final warning (*CR v AD* [2000] Crim LR 867). Persistence can be established on a first conviction even in the absence of previous reprimands and warnings. For example in *R v Smith* ([2000] Crim LR 613) a 14-year-old boy who had participated in three robberies, two offensive weapons offences and a false imprisonment in a 24 hour period was held to be a persistent offender. However the test of persistence will not be satisfied simply because the offender has committed more than one offence, particularly where the offences vary in character. *R v ID* ((2000) unreported case no. 200015005174) suggested that persistence will be more readily found where the offender has repeated the same kind of offending.

A custodial sentence of detention, without the training component, can only be passed to those aged 18, 19 or 20 years. However for grave crimes the youth court can pass its jurisdiction to the Crown Court. Grave crimes will be examined in more detail in Chapter 12. As a condition of the community period of the DTO, the court can require the young person to be on an intensive supervision and surveillance programme (ISSP). The ISSP combines community-based surveillance with a comprehensive and sustained focus on tackling the factors that contribute to the young persons offending behaviour. ISSPs target the most persistent and serious offenders. An ISSP can be used as a condition of bail or as an adjunct to a community or custodial sentence for serious offenders or persistent young offenders who at the time of appearing in court have previously been charged, warned or convicted on four or more separate occasions in the preceding 12 months and have previously received at least one community or custodial sentence. An ISSP runs for a maximum of six months with intensive supervision (including electronic tagging) and engagement (for example education or vocational training, offending behaviour programmes and recreational activities) for 25 hours a week for the first three months.

The detention and training order was heralded as a measure to ensure that custody for children was a constructive experience with an appropriate focus on education and training (Home Office, 1997a; Youth Justice Board, 2000). The rationale behind the order is the belief that the increased emphasis on supervision after release, a clear sentence plan to tackle the underlying causes of offending and on community supervision after release from custody would provide a 'clearer, simpler, more flexible and more consistent custodial arrangement for young offenders' (Home Office, 1997a: 6.20). However it represents a substantial increase in the custodial powers of the youth court and a loosening of the conditions which must be satisfied before custodial orders can be imposed on children aged between 12 and 14 years (NACRO, 2000b). Courts can impose a detention and training order on offenders as young as 10 years. Moreover section 130 of the Criminal Justice and Police Act 2001 grants the courts new powers to remand into secure accommodation persistent young offenders aged 12–16 years. The 2001 Act empowers the courts to remand children to custodial institutions in cases where they have repeatedly committed offences while on bail irrespective of whether or not such offences are adjudged to expose the public to serious harm. The term repeatedly has been defined in case law as meaning on more than one occasion. Thus section 130 of the 2001 Act has effectively replaced the long established 'seriousness' threshold with a nuisance test (Goldson, 2006).

## Custodial institutions

Three types of institution are available to hold young offenders:

(1)  *Secure children's homes* – These are local authority secure accommodation run by social services (rather than the prison estate) and are available for offenders up to the age of 16 years, and are generally used for those aged 12–14 years. Secure children's homes house both young offenders and vulnerable young people, and focus on intensive one-on-one work with young people to address their behavioural problems. However the Secure children's home can refuse to take any young offenders from the youth court. Secure children's homes focus on attending to the physical, emotional and behavioural needs of the young people they accommodate.

(2)  *Secure training centres (STC)* – These are part of the prison estate and there are only four such units, holding no more than 50 young people at any time. They are located in Milton Keynes, Durham, Northamptonshire and Kent. There is a comparably high staff/inmate ratio and they aim to provide a more constructive and educational regime. They provide a tailored

programme for young people that allows them the opportunity to develop as individuals and stop them reoffending. Trainees are provided with formal education for 25 hours a week, 52 weeks of the year.

(3) *Young offender institutions (YOI)* – These are a more traditional prison environment with a capacity to hold large numbers. They generally have a lower ratio of staff to young people and accommodate larger numbers of young people than secure training centres and secure children's homes. Consequently they are less able to address the individual needs of young people.

It is not for the court to place the young offender; this will be decided by the Youth Justice Board. In *R (on the application of SR) v Nottingham Magistrates' Court* ([2001] EWHC Admin 802) Lord Brooke held that when assessing the appropriateness of placing a 16-year-old boy in a young offender institution, Article 3(1) of the United Nations Convention on the Rights of the Child should apply. Thus every public authority concerned with issues relating to the care and management of children must consider the best interests of the child as a primary consideration in line with Article 3(1) of the UN Convention and ensure that it applies to every child without discrimination in accordance with Article 2(1) of the Convention. This case establishes a positive duty upon relevant authorities to guarantee that minimum safeguards are adhered to in order to protect the welfare of young people in custody. Such a view was also expressed in the case of *R (on the application of the Howard League for Penal Reform) v Secretary of State for the Home Department and the Department of Health* ([2002] EWHC 2497). In this case Munby J held that the child protection provisions of the Children Act 1989 and the 'welfare' principle encapsulated in Article 3 of the UN Convention did not cease to apply to a child in a young offender institution. The court held that these principles should operate subject to the requirements of custody, but always having regard to:

1   the principle that the best interests of the child are at all times a primary consideration;
2   the inherent vulnerability of children in a young offender institution; and
3   the need for the state to take effective deterrent steps to prevent, and to provide children in young offender institutions with effective protection from, ill-treatment (whether at the hands of Prison Service staff or of other inmates) of which the Prison Service has or ought to have knowledge.

The Children Act 2004 set out a new framework of law covering safeguarding arrangements for all children, with those in custody being specifically provided for in the legislation. The Act places a responsibility to safeguard and promote the welfare of children on all managers of secure facilities; and governors or directors of secure establishments are required to act as partners in the new Local Safeguarding Children Boards. The Youth Justice Board's code of practice *Managing Children and Young People's Behaviour in the Secure Estate* (February 2006) makes it clear that restraint should only be undertaken on the basis of a risk assessment that harm is likely to occur if a physical intervention is not employed. The Youth Justice Board has set up a joint behaviour management/safeguarding programme board with the prison service which will consider a number of policy areas impacting on behaviour management.

## Does custody work?

Article 37 of the United Nations Convention on the Rights of the Child states that custody of a child 'shall only be used as a measure of last resort and for the shortest appropriate period of time'. However in England and Wales, age reductions in the detention of young people coupled with increases in maximum sentence appear directly to be at odds with the requirements of the UN Convention. A study by the children's charity Barnardos of the cases of 214 children aged between 12 and 14 years and sentenced to detention and training orders found that 35 per cent of the sample did not meet the criteria for custody as they had not committed a serious offence and were not persistent offenders (Glover and Hibbert, 2009). The report also found that 22 per cent of the sample was sent to custody for breaching a community sentence penalty. Based on Glover and Hibbert's report, Barnardos have recommended that the government develop strict sentencing rules with a clear definition of persistency so that custody is reserved only for those who warrant it and that a breach of a community sentence should never result in imprisonment unless the breach has involved violence or further serious offending.

   The practice of imprisoning children also appears to run counter to the aim of preventing offending. The vast majority of young people in custody pose no danger or risk to the community. Indeed they may be a significantly greater danger on their return. When a young person is in custody they are making no reparation to the victim or society. Child imprisonment makes little if any positive effect in preventing offending: patterns of reconviction with regard to children, following release from all forms of custodial institution are exceptionally high (Goldson, 2005: 82). Hagell and Hazell (2001) also noted with concern that child imprisonment compounds the likelihood of reconviction and that this has been a recurrent and enduring historical theme of youth imprisonment. Indeed Mary Carpenter described prisons as the 'most costly, most inefficacious for any end but to prepare the child for a life of crime' (Carpenter, 1853: 13). This view was echoed by the government in the early 1990s when it described custody as 'an expensive way of making bad people worse', reflecting the government's concern about the cost and effectiveness of custody (Home Office, 1990: 27). As Miller stated, 'the hard truth is that . . . juvenile penal institutions have minimal impact on crime [and if] most prisons were closed tomorrow, the rise in crime would be negligible (Miller, 1991: 181–2).

The prevalence of violence in young offender institutions is well established. O'Donnell and Edgar (1996) concluded that 46 per cent of all young people in custody had been 'assaulted, robbed or threatened with violence'. The Howard League (2001: 8) reported that between April 2000 and March 2001 93 per cent of young people at Castington Young Offender Institution had been assaulted. Where bullying led to self-harm, then staff were likely to regard such behaviour as attention seeking (Howard League, 2001: 14). During an unannounced inspection of Feltham Young Offender Institution, the Chief Inspector of Prisons found that young people in the unit 'had not been unlocked for five days, other than to collect their meals' (Chief Inspector of HM Prisons, 1999: 1.90) and that a 16 year old who was in custody for the first time was sharing a cell with a 20 year old on remand for serious violent offences. The inspection of Feltham concluded that 'cells and common areas were . . . dilapidated, dirty and cold . . . . Bedding and linen were unwashed and in a poor state of repair . . . boys continued to eat in dirty cells with filthy toilets' (Chief Inspector of HM Prisons, 1999: 1.02–1.04). A 2009 inspection of a young offender institution at Cookham Wood in Kent found that inmates refused to leave their cells, even to eat, through fears for their safety (Chief Inspector of HM Prisons, 2009). Conditions were found to be seriously unsafe as too many inmates had been put there. The report also identified a 'tense' relationship between staff and inmates at the facility. Such conditions are in violation of the UN Convention requirement that when deprived of liberty, children should be treated with humanity. Goldson (2005: 85) is in no doubt that there exists a credible case for the abolition of child incarceration, a process which 'systematically harms and damages children: physically, emotionally and psychologically'.

It seems that governments and policy makers are only prepared to sanction preventive measures as long as custody is retained for particular groups of young offenders. There are clear grounds for investing heavily in prevention; as a report on young offender institutions put it: 'if you select at random any inmate of a Young Offenders' Institution, you will almost certainly find a heartbreaking history of personal misery, professional neglect and lost opportunities' (Rethinking Crime and Punishment and Children's Rights Alliance for England, 2002). The Audit Commission (2004) calculated that if effective early intervention had been provided for just one in ten of these young offenders, annual savings in excess of £100 million could have been made.

The current approach to using custody in the English youth justice system fails to address the underlying causes of offending, does not prevent offending and is very expensive. Expenditure on custody accounts for almost 70 per cent of the Youth Justice Board's expenditure. A greater use

*Table 10.2* History of custody

| | |
|---|---|
| 1838 | Parkhurst prison for boys |
| 1854 | Youthful Offenders Act provided for the reformatory |
| 1857 | Industrial Schools Act introduced the industrial schools |
| 1908 | Prevention of Crime Act introduced borstals |
| 1933 | Children and Young Persons Act replaced reformatories and industrial schools with approved schools |
| 1948 | Criminal Justice Act established remand centres and detention centres |
| 1982 | Criminal Justice Act established youth custody centres |
| 1988 | Criminal Justice Act replaced detention centres and youth custody centres with young offender institutions |
| 1994 | Criminal Justice and Public Order Act established secure training centres |
| 1998 | Crime and Disorder Act replaced young offender institutions and secure training centres with detention and training centres |

of community sentences would be more cost effective with the possibility of steering less serious offenders away from custody and offending. Community sentences offer a more effective sentence than custody and allow the offender to put something back into the community. This is a view echoed by the European Commission of Human Rights. The Commission noted that in the English youth justice system 'juvenile trouble-makers are too rapidly drawn into the criminal justice system . . . and too readily placed in detention, when greater attention to alternate forms of supervision and targeted early intervention would be more effective' (European Commission, 2005: 81).

---

### Discussion topic

'Prison sentences are not succeeding in turning the majority of offenders away from crime' (Social Exclusion Unit, 2002: 1). Do you think this view can be applied to the incarceration of young people?

---

*Comment*

It has long been maintained that the great majority of young people sentenced to custody pose no serious risk to the community, and, indeed, by leading to broken links with family, friends, education, work and leisure they may become a significantly greater danger on their return. Moreover, custody diverts considerable resources from community provision to high security institutions. These institutions are beset with brutality, suicide, self-harm and barbaric conditions.

The case against custody:

- Custody fails to prevent reoffending or to act as a deterrent. Over 80 per cent of those sent to youth custody reoffend within a two year period following release.
- A young person in custody is making no reparation to the victim or society.
- Custody is a very expensive option, diverting resources from prevention programmes.
- Article 37 of the United Nations Convention on the Rights of the Child states that custody of a child 'shall only be used as a measure of last resort and for the shortest appropriate period of time'. In England, age reductions in the detention of young people coupled with increases in maximum sentence appear directly at odds with this.
- Custodial institutions are so dire and abusive that they infringe the young person's human rights.
- Education and vocational training within young offender institutions is inadequate; very little help is provided with post-release settlement.

## Suggested further reading

Bateman, T. (2005) 'Reducing child imprisonment: a systematic challenge', *Youth Justice*, 5, 2, 91–105.

Drakeford, M. and Butler, I. (2007) 'Everyday Tragedies: Justice, Scandal and Young People in Contemporary Britain', *Howard Journal of Criminal Justice*, 46, 3, 219–35.

Goldson, B. (2005) 'Child imprisonment: a case for abolition', *Youth Justice*, 5, 77.

# 11 Punishing parents for youth offending

## Introduction

When sentencing convicted young offenders, the youth court has the option of punishing the young person's parents for the incidence of youth offending. This chapter examines the laws which hold parents responsible for their children's offending. It examines the history of parental responsibility laws in England and Wales, discusses the role of parental responsibility laws in the current youth justice system and analyses any problems which such laws may potentially pose.

## History of parental responsibility laws

Enforcing parental responsibility for youth offending has been a characteristic feature of the history of youth crime control since the nineteenth century. As you will recall from Chapter 1, the Youthful Offenders Act 1854 permitted the setting up of reformatory schools by voluntary societies to contain and morally reeducate 'deviant' children. The 1854 Act also required parents to pay maintenance while their children were in the reformatory schools. This measure was intended to enforce parental responsibility. The establishment of industrial schools also ensured that parents were required to contribute to the maintenance of their children. Children found begging or who had no visible means of subsistence were deemed to be beyond parental control and could be sent to an industrial school indefinitely, under the Industrial Schools Act 1857. From 1857, parents were to pay five shillings a week if they could afford it. The burden of maintenance created an incentive for parents to conform to the dominant middle class child-rearing practices (Muncie 1999). Parental shortcomings were thus viewed as a fundamental cause of youth offending behaviour and the state aimed to compel responsible behaviour on the part of parents. The Children and Young Persons Act 1933 was the first Act to empower the courts to require parents to pay the fines of a young offender. Section 55 of the 1933 Act provided that the parent need not pay their child's fine if they had not conduced the commission of the offence by neglecting to exercise due care and control. The Criminal Justice Act 1982 introduced a presumption that parents should be made responsible for their children's offending behaviour. The 1982 Act allowed courts to order parents to pay a young offender's fines or compensation. Accordingly, by the time of the Criminal Justice Act 1991 specific measures were available which allowed for the imposition of financial penalties upon parents when crimes were committed by their children.

In a White Paper published in February 1990, the government expressed its intention to take further measures to enforce parents' responsibility for the criminal acts of their children aged between 10 and 16 years (Home Office, 1990). Originally it wanted to make it a criminal offence for parents to 'fail to prevent their children from committing offences'. However this proposal was heavily criticised by, among others, the Magistrates' Association and was subsequently dropped. The main criticisms were that most young offenders' lives are characterised by economic and social disadvantage, family breakdown and a lack of a positive role model such as an appropriate father figure. It was argued that resources could better be diverted to helping such families through education and social work support. It was further argued that the proposal was likely to be counterproductive in that it might lead to the complete disintegration of already fragile family units (West, 1982). Despite these criticisms, the first law in England and Wales which held parents directly responsible, as opposed to financially liable, was enshrined in the Criminal Justice Act 1991. Section 58 of the 1991 Act requires a parent to accompany to court any of their children, aged between 10 and 16 years and accused of a criminal offence, and to pay any fine and/or costs. The most significant aspect of the 1991 Act was the introduction of the parental 'bind over'. The parent could be 'bound over' by the court to exercise control over an offending child. Failure to meet the terms of the bind over could result in a fine of £1,000. The Criminal Justice and Public Order Act 1994 extended this power to include parents having to ensure their child's compliance with the requirements of a community sentence. This is the first time that parents have been fined for their failure to control their children's behaviour. In relation to a young person between 10 and 16 years of age, this power must be exercised where the court is satisfied that it would be desirable in the interests of preventing the commission of further offences by the offender (section 150(1) Powers of Criminal Courts (Sentencing) Act 2000). If the court is not satisfied that it would be appropriate to impose a bind over on the parents of an offender under 16 years, it must state openly why it is of this opinion (section 150(1)(a) Powers of Criminal Courts (Sentencing) Act 2000).

The Crime and Disorder Act 1998 built upon this principle of parental responsibility by introducing the 'parenting order' enabling the court to require the parent of every convicted young offender to attend parenting programmes and if necessary to control the future behaviour of the young person in a specified manner. The parenting programmes deal with issues such as experiences of parenting, communication and negotiation skills, parenting style and the importance of consistency, praise and rewards, and can include a residential element. In effect, the parenting order requires a parent to attend counselling or guidance sessions once a week for a maximum of 12 weeks. Parents may also be required to apply control over their child, for example they may be ordered to ensure their child attends school or avoids associating with particular individuals who are adversely affecting their behaviour. Section 8 of the 1998 Act outlines the circumstances in which the court may impose a parenting order: where a child safety order has been made in respect of a child; where an anti-social behaviour order, or sex offender order, is made on a child or young person; where a person is convicted of an offence under section 443 (failure to comply with a school attendance order) or section 444 (failure to secure regular attendance at school of registered pupil) of the Education Act 1996; or where a referral order has been made. The relevant condition that has to be satisfied to justify making a parenting order is that the order is desirable in the interests of preventing any repetition of the kind of behaviour that led to the order being made and the prevention of further offending by the child or young person. Before issuing a parenting order the court should consider the family's circumstances and the likely impact of such an order on those circumstances (section 9(2) Crime and Disorder Act 1998). Should a parent fail to comply with the requirements of the order they may be liable to a fine of up to £1,000. In 1997 the Home Office consultation paper *Tackling Youth Crime* first detailed the underlying principle of the parenting order, which was to make 'parents who wilfully neglected their responsibilities answerable to the court' (Home Office, 1997b: 32). This consultation paper was followed by the White Paper *No More Excuses: A New Approach to Tackling Youth Crime in England and Wales* (Home Office, 1997a) which stated that the government intended to make parents more responsible for their children's behaviour by making available sanctions for parents who evade their responsibilities.

The Anti-Social Behaviour Act 2003 perpetuates the statutory assumption that parents of children who offend have not accepted their responsibility and that they can be made to do so by the imposition of court orders and financial penalties. Section 87(3) of the 2003 Act allows for the issuing of Fixed Penalty Notices to parents of offenders between the ages of 10 and 16 years. The Anti-Social Behaviour Act also increases the circumstances in which a parenting order can be made. Section 26 empowers youth offending teams (YOTs) to apply to the courts for parenting orders where the YOT suspects that the parent is not taking active steps to prevent the child's anti-social or criminal-type behaviour, and it is clear that this behaviour will continue. Local education authorities will also be able to seek a parenting order where a child has been excluded from school for serious misbehaviour. Accordingly parents who have not committed any crime can receive a parenting order in response to their children who have not committed any crime (Holt, 2008: 204).

Section 144 of the Serious Organised Crime and Police Act 2005 introduced parental compensation orders. A parental compensation order is a civil order which requires a parent to compensate, up to a maximum of £5,000, any person whose property has been taken or damaged by their child. Such an order may be made by a magistrate where a child under 10 years of age has taken or has caused loss or damage to property in the course of acting in either an anti-social manner or in a way which would have been a criminal offence had the child been over 10 years of age. A parental compensation order can only be made if it would be desirable in the interests of preventing repetition of the offending behaviour. Section 137 of the Powers of the Criminal Courts (Sentencing) Act 2000 provides that in the case of a child under 16 years of age, a criminal compensation order that has been made under section 130 must be paid by the parent, unless the parent cannot be found or it would be unreasonable to do so. When the child is aged between 16 and 17 years then the power to make the order against the parent is discretionary.

Section 24 of the Police and Justice Act 2006 allows registered social landlords to apply for a parenting order where they have reason to believe that a child is engaged in anti-social behaviour. Registered social landlords provide low cost housing for people in housing need. Parenting orders can thus be made even where a child has not committed an offence, been charged with an offence or been issued with an ASBO. In the case of *R(M) v Inner London Crown Court* ([2003] EWHC 301 Admin) it was ruled that parenting orders did not infringe the European Convention on Human Rights. The court held that although the parenting order was an infringement of family life, and thus potentially violated Article 8 of the European Convention, it was justified as a necessary and proportionate infringement. Also the court held that the parenting order does not breach the right to a fair trial, enshrined in Article 6, as it is based on evaluation rather than a particular standard of proof.

## Parenting orders in practice

Parenting orders offer parents the opportunity to develop their parenting skills. However, are they effective in changing young people's behaviour and encouraging young people to desist from further offending behaviour? Ghate and Ramella evaluated the effectiveness of parenting programmes in a study involving 800 parents and 500 young people (Ghate and Ramella, 2002). The researchers found significant evidence of positive change in parents who participated in the programmes, including improved supervision and monitoring of their children's activities, a reduction in the frequency of conflict with their children and an improved ability to cope with parenting in general. There was also evidence of positive change for young people during the time their parents participated in the programme. Young people reported improved supervision and monitoring by their parents, reduction in the frequency of conflict with their parents and improved relationship with their parents. In the year after the parents left the programme, the reconviction rates of young people had fallen by over 30 per cent, offending had dropped by 56 per cent and the average number of offences per young person reduced by 50 per cent. The evidence suggests that the parenting programme helped to slow down young people's anti-social and offending behaviour. Scott *et al.*'s study also showed that parenting programmes improved several aspects of parenting in important ways such as increasing sensitive responding to children, improving the use of effective discipline and decreasing criticism (Scott *et al.* 2006). The study showed that the intervention had lasting effects on the parent–child relationship for at least six months after the intervention had ended. This evidence relates to parenting programmes in general; many of the participants will have been there voluntarily. While the supportive aspects of the parenting order are attractive, evidence indicates that using compulsion and the threat of fines and imprisonment is not an effective way to change the behaviour of parents and their children. According to Ghate and Ramella's evaluation of parenting programmes, voluntary participants were more likely to have positive expectations of the intervention than those whose attendance was court-ordered, who were less likely to have found the programme helpful (Ghate and Ramella, 2002). Field found in his interviews with a range of youth justice practitioners in Wales that many YOTs in Wales had marginalised parenting orders. Parenting orders were generally seen as being unhelpfully coercive and so YOTs discouraged magistrates from using them where parents had not agreed to participate voluntarily (Field, 2007).

## Problems with parenting orders

Laws that penalise parents for their children's behaviour ignore the complex patterns and interrelated problems that such families invariably endure. These laws cast parents as 'failures' and confront them with the prospect of financial penalties and potentially imprisonment. The parental responsibility laws exacerbate the impact of risk factors in the lives of youth at greatest risk of offending. The criminological research suggests that in many cases where children are in trouble, the reality of parenthood undoubtedly involves vulnerability and poverty, with many parents (especially mothers) living on state benefits and experiencing housing problems. Thus the parents punished for 'failing' are likely to be striving to hold their family together in the face of severe pressures. Parental responsibility laws are unlikely to ameliorate any of the damaging family conditions which induce young people into offending behaviour; indeed, these laws fail to address the underlying problems and serve to deepen divisions and further alienate vulnerable families. They lead to strains in families where relationships are already tense and fragile and they convert parents and children into adversarial parties in the home. Punishing parents for a perceived lack of responsibility on their part accelerates family conflict and breakdown. For example these measures aggravate the poverty that lies behind so much anti-social behaviour. Fining parents deprives not only the child whose conduct triggered the court action but also any siblings of at least some measure of the parents' financial and personal support.

Parental responsibility laws contradict fundamental principles of criminal liability (Commission on Families and Wellbeing of Children, 2005; Hollingsworth, 2007b). Customarily a crime requires proof of a physical act (*actus reus*) and the requisite mental state (*mens rea*). The accused must have either acted voluntarily or failed to act under circumstances imposing a duty to act. Parental responsibility laws enforce a form of strict liability on parents, in that parents are liable even if they exercised reasonable care. The court does not need to prove that the parents were at fault to make the order. The parent has not been convicted of any offence, and in some circumstances the child may not have been convicted of any offence, but both parent and child are subject to sanction.

Parental responsibility laws serve to fragment the government's approach to both tackling youth crime and supporting families in crisis. In 1997 the government stated in *No More Excuses* that 'as they develop, children must bear an increasing responsibility for their actions, just as the responsibility of parents gradually declines' (Home Office, 1997a). The government believed that to prevent offending and reoffending by young people, society must stop making excuses for youth crime. According to this view children above the age of criminal responsibility are generally mature enough to be held accountable for their actions and the law should recognise this. Yet parental responsibility laws are built upon the idea that parents have caused their children to offend. Rather than parental responsibility decreasing when the child is held criminally responsible, both parent and child are held legally liable regardless of the actual or indeed presumed capacity of the child, and consequently there is no diminution in parental responsibility as the child gains responsibility (Hollingsworth, 2007b).

Parental responsibility is frequently left to mothers, thus parental responsibility orders can operate as 'mothering orders' (Holt, 2009: 344) enabling a formalised state to use a blunt instrument to target mothers. The parenting order assumes that the parent, usually the mother, can exercise control over their child ignoring the difficulties that a mother may experience in controlling the behaviour of a young man.

Parental responsibility laws also infringe some of Britain's obligations under international law. Article 18.2 of the United Nations Convention on the Rights of the Child sets out the obligations of the state to assist parents in raising their children: ' . . . States Parties shall render appropriate assistance to parents and legal guardians in the performance of their child-rearing responsibilities and shall ensure the development of institutions, facilities and services for the care of children.' Article 1.2 of the United

Nations Rules on the Administration of Juvenile Justice (the Beijing Rules) 1985 stresses the idea that the state should ensure a productive life for young people within the community such as to encourage in them a process of personal development and education 'during that period in life when she or he is most susceptible to deviant behaviour'. The 1990 Riyadh Guidelines emphasise that policies should avoid criminalising and penalising a child for behaviour that does not cause serious damage to the development of the child or to others. The Riyadh Guidelines stress that the successful prevention of juvenile delinquency requires efforts on the part of the entire society to ensure the harmonious development of adolescents with respect for, and promotion of, their personality from early childhood. By engaging in lawful, socially-useful activities and adopting a humanistic orientation towards society, young people can develop non-criminogenic attitudes. The Riyadh Guidelines recommend that policies and measures should involve the provision of opportunities to meet the varying needs of young people and to serve as a supportive framework for safeguarding the personal development of all young people, particularly those who are demonstrably endangered or at social risk and are in need of special care and protection. The Guidelines support preventive policies which facilitate the successful socialisation and integration of all young people, in particular through the family. Article 33 states that 'Communities should provide ... a wide range of community-based support measures for young persons, including community development centres, recreational facilities and services designed in view of the special problems of children in a situation of social risk.'

The Convention on the Rights of the Child, the Beijing rules and the Riyadh Guidelines point to the important role that a constructive social policy for juveniles could play in the prevention of youth offending. In addition to this wealth of UN material, the child's right to protection from involvement in anti-social and offending behaviour can be found in instruments of the Council of Europe. In 1987 Recommendation R(87)20, on social reactions to juvenile delinquency, was adopted by the Committee of Ministers of the Council of Europe. The Council of Europe recommended that each of the member states review their legislation and practices in view of putting into practice a global policy of prevention of maladjustment and delinquency. Similar to the various United Nations rules and resolutions, this Recommendation places emphasis on the role of the family and society in the treatment of young people. Furthermore in 1996 the Council of Europe adopted a European strategy for children urging member states to fully implement the United Nations Convention as well as relevant European Conventions to ensure children's rights (Parliamentary Assembly of Europe, Recommendation 1286, 1996). Although the recommendations of the Council of Europe are not legally binding they are adopted unanimously and so carry weight and indicate a common approach to policy and minimum standards (Van Beuren, 1992).

The philosophy that directs the general principles of the United Nations

Convention, Rules and Guidelines, as well as the European recommendations and strategies, is essentially based on the protection of the personality of all young people below 18 years of age and on the mobilisation of existing resources within the community. These instruments of international law emphasise the need for prevention policies and interventions to avoid a narrow focus on the crime and to take into account the family, social and contextual factors that are frequently associated with juvenile offending.

*Table 11.1* The history of parental responsibility laws in England and Wales

| | |
|---|---|
| Youthful Offenders Act 1854 | Required parents to pay maintenance while their children were in the reformatory schools. |
| Industrial Schools Act 1857 | Parents were to pay five shillings a week, if they could afford it, as a contribution to the maintenance of their children while in industrial schools. |
| Children and Young Persons Act 1933 | Required parents to pay the fines of a young offender. |
| Criminal Justice Act 1982 | Courts could order parents to pay a young offender's fines or compensation. |
| Criminal Justice Act 1991 | Requires a parent to accompany to court any of their children and to pay any fine and/or costs. Introduced the parental 'bind over', which allowed the courts to order the parent to exercise control over an offending child. |
| Criminal Justice and Public Order Act 1994 | Extended the parental bind over to allow the courts to order the parents to ensure their child's compliance with the requirements of a community sentence. |
| Crime and Disorder Act 1998 | Introduced the parenting order, enabling the court to require the parent of every convicted young offender to attend parenting programmes and if necessary to control the future behaviour of the young person in a specified manner. |
| Powers of Criminal Courts (Sentencing) Act 2000 | The courts must exercise the parental bind over in relation to a young person between 10 and 16 years of age, where the court is satisfied that it would be desirable in the interests of preventing the commission of further offending. |
| The Anti-Social Behaviour Act 2003 | Empowers youth offending teams to apply to the courts for parenting orders. Allows for the issuing of Fixed Penalty Notices to parents of young offenders. |
| Serious Organised Crime and Police Act 2005 | Introduced the parental compensation order which requires a parent to compensate any person whose property has been taken or damaged by their child. |
| Police and Justice Act 2006 | Allows registered social landlords to apply for a parenting order where they have reason to believe that a child is engaged in anti-social behaviour. |

They promote the principle that in order to reduce the risk some children face of becoming offenders, the best strategy is to promote positive life and family experiences for all children, and not to penalise families. They recognise that sometimes parents need extra support to give them the skills and confidence to address their children's behaviour problems and that help should be provided to families where they need it.

Statutory parenting interventions that are of relatively short duration and which come at a comparatively late stage in young people's lives are unlikely to offer a quick fix for the complex circumstances that might give rise to criminal or anti-social behaviour (Goldson and Jamieson 2002). Instead such interventions are likely to place further stress on families which are close to breaking point. The parental responsibility laws oversimplify the complex linkage between parenting and delinquency in a reductionist effort to blame parents for their children's wrongs. A change in political vision has to be made from short term and supposed immediate gains to one in which long term investment in the lives of children is accepted. Rather than penalising families, youth justice policy should seek to reduce youth crime by improving the life chances for the young people in our communities. Programs that strengthen the family and foster healthy growth and development of children from prenatal care through adolescence should replace policies which seek to penalise and punish struggling families.

---

### Discussion topic

How has the development of notions of childhood affected the way in which the law responds to the parents of young offenders?

---

*Comment*

Parental responsibility laws are based on the assumption that parents of children who offend have not accepted their responsibility and that they can be made to do so by the imposition of court orders and financial penalties. This view of parents being responsible for their children's offences is one that has found favour throughout history. For example, Aristotle asserted that in order to be virtuous 'we ought to have been brought up in a particular way from our very youth'. Diogenes of Sinope believed that 'if the child swears, slap the parent'. Notions of 'good' and 'bad' parenting have informed much of the youth justice system's response to youth crime since the nineteenth century. However an image of willfully negligent parents colluding with or even encouraging misbehaviour was popularised in the 1980s and 90s. The breakdown of the nuclear family unit, high divorce rates and increases in single parenting, it was argued, were the root causes of moral decay epitomised by increased crime rates, homelessness and drug abuse. In addition, excessive welfare dependency encouraged families to rely on state benefits rather than on each other, and in this process children's moral development has been eroded. As a result, since the 1980s successive governments have introduced a series of measures to enforce parents to bring up their children responsibly. Single parenting, teenage mothers and absent fathers are key harbingers of social disorder. The weak family is viewed as the key driver of crime. 'Weak' families are those with poor parenting skills, teenage pregnancies, single parenting and broken homes. Strong families are now seen as the centre of peaceful and safe communities. Respect is all important and this is missing from dysfunctional families. In this rhetoric, strong families fit the traditional image of conjugal, heterosexual parents with an employed male breadwinner.

## Suggested further reading

Burney, E. and Gelsthorpe, L. (2008) 'Do we need a "naughty step"? Rethinking the parenting order after ten years', *The Howard Journal of Criminal Justice*, 47, 5, 470–85.

Hollingsworth, K. (2007) 'Responsibility and Rights: Children and their Parents in the Youth Justice System', *International Journal of Law, Policy and the Family*, 21, 2, 190–219.

Koffman, L. (2008) 'Holding parents to account: tough on children, tough on the causes of children?', *Journal of Law and Society*, 35, 1, 113–30.

# 12 Youth offending cases in the adult Crown Court

## Introduction

The majority of criminal cases against those aged under 18 years are tried and sentenced in the youth court. Cases involving young offenders will only appear in the adult Crown Court in a limited number of specific circumstances. One such circumstance is where the young person has committed a homicide or a grave crime, defined as an offence punishable with 14 years imprisonment or more in the case of an adult offender. Similarly, where a young person has committed an offence with an adult offender, they may both be referred to the Crown Court. Thus a youth will only appear in the Crown Court for trial and sentence when: charged with homicide; charged with a grave crime; or when charged together with an adult offender who has been sent to the Crown Court. For homicide cases there is no discretion, the youth must be sent to the Crown Court. In the other circumstances, the court has a discretion to send a case to the Crown Court if it is considered appropriate. Chapter 12 will examine the manner in which young people are tried in the Crown Court.

## Trial of young person in the Crown Court

As already stated, most criminal cases involving young people will be heard in the youth court. You will recall from Chapter 10 that the maximum custodial penalty which the youth court can impose is a 24 month detention and training order (DTO). However longer periods of detention may be imposed on a young person sentenced in the Crown Court.

There are a number of circumstances in which a young person might appear in the adult Crown Court. If a child is jointly charged with an adult, the case will commence in the adult court. The young person's trial may take place with the adult in the adult Crown Court if it is considered to be in the interests of justice. Where the offence is considered to be a 'grave offence' then the case may be tried in the adult Crown Court. Grave crimes are defined in sections 90–92 of the Powers of Criminal Courts (Sentencing) Act 2000 as including:

- murder;
- an offence which if committed by an adult would be punishable with imprisonment of more than 14 years;
- sexual assault;
- child sex offences;
- sexual activity with a family member or inciting a family member to engage in sexual activity;
- possession of or distributing prohibited weapons or ammunition;
- possessing or distributing a firearm disguised as another object.

All of the above attract sentences longer than the 24 month DTO which the youth court can impose and this automatically takes the offences beyond the sentencing powers of the youth court and within the scope of 'grave crimes' to be tried and sentenced by the Crown Court. In the case of murder the case must be tried in the Crown Court. Also in the case of the firearms offences, if the young person is aged over 16 years then a Crown Court trial will be mandatory. For all of the other grave crimes the youth court must decide whether to accept the case or refer it for trial to the Crown Court. The youth court's decision will be based on which court can pass the most appropriate sentence if the young person is convicted. In the case of *R (on the application of W) v Thetford Youth Court and R (on the application of M) v Waltham Forest Youth Court* ([2002] EWHC 1252 (Admin)) the High Court held that referral to the Crown Court should be 'very much a long stop, reserved for very serious offences'. Gage J held that unless the offence merits a sentence of custody longer than two years then the youth court should deal with the offender by means of a DTO or by non-custodial means. Sedley LJ believed that referral to the Crown Court should only ever be a 'last resort' as the trial of a child in public, before a jury of adults in a contested case, is a far from insignificant contrast with trial in a youth court. In *R (on the application of W) v Southampton Youth Court and R (on the application of K) v Wirral Youth Court* ([2002] EWHC 1640 (Admin)), the High Court further held that a case should only be referred to the Crown Court if there is a real possibility that a penalty of two years or more would be appropriate. In this case the High Court overturned a youth court decision to commit three 13-year-old boys for trial in the Crown Court for indecently assaulting another 13-year-old boy. The High Court held that given the ages of the boys the case was not at the level of a two year custodial sentence. The High Court recommended that the case be tried in the youth court and if convicted a non-custodial sentence should be imposed as none of the boys were persistent offenders.

Youth offending cases can also be tried in the Crown Court if the case involves a violent or sexual offence, as specified in Schedule 15 of the Criminal Justice Act 2003. Such cases may go to the Crown Court if the youth court considers that the young person might reasonably be considered 'dangerous'. Dangerousness will exist where the court determines that there is a significant risk of serious harm caused by the young person committing another of the offences specified in the 2003 Act (NACRO, 2006). In *R v Lang and others* ([2005] EWCA Crim 2864) the Court of Appeal provided detailed guidance on defining dangerousness in cases involving young people. The risk of serious harm is to 'members of the public' and can include particular groups such as prison officers or hospital staff for example. The risk identified must be 'noteworthy, of considerable amount or importance'. The Court should take account of current and previous offending, their circumstances, sentences passed, social factors such as employment, education, accommodation, family relationships, drug or alcohol use, the young person's attitude to supervision and their emotional state. In *Lang* the Court held that a likelihood of committing a serious specified offence does not automatically mean that there is a signifi- cant risk of serious harm as there may be a significant risk of further offending but not of serious harm. The Court of Appeal stressed the impor- tance of considering the rate of maturity and development when assessing whether there is a risk of serious harm.

## The Crown Court trial

The trial of young people in the Crown Court is governed by the *Consolidated Criminal Practice Direction 2007*. The overriding principle of the Practice Direction is that the trial process should not expose young people to avoidable intimidation, humiliation or distress, and that regard should be had to the welfare principle as stated in section 44 of the Children and Young Persons Act 1933. The Practice Direction directs that the trial should, if practicable, be held in a courtroom in which all the participants are on the same or almost the same level. The young person should usually be free to sit with members of their family in a place which permits easy, informal communication with legal representatives and others with whom the young person may need to communicate. The Practice Direction requires the court to take account of the defendant's age and maturity and of their ability to understand what is going on when making arrangements for trial. The language used should be comprehensible by the young person, robes and wigs should not be worn and there should be no recognizable police presence in the courtroom. Despite these provisions the United Nations Committee on the Rights of the Child have been critical of English law which allows for children to be processed in the adult courts and recom- mended that steps be taken to ensure that 'no child can be tried as an adult, irrespective of the circumstances, or the gravity of [the] offence' (United Nations Committee on the Rights of the Child, 2002).

## The killing of James Bulger in Liverpool in 1993

On Friday 12 February 1993 two-year-old James Bulger went on a shopping trip with his mother Denise in Liverpool. During this shopping trip James was abducted by Robert Thompson and Jon Venables, both aged 10 years. Thompson and Venables then walked James three miles to a section of railway track. During the entire walk the two boys and James were seen by 38 people, some of whom noticed an injury to James' head and later recalled that he seemed distressed. Others reported that James appeared happy and was seen laughing, the boys seemingly alternating between hurting and distracting him. At the railway track, one of the boys threw blue modelling paint on James' face. They kicked him and hit him with bricks, stones and a 22lb (10kg) iron bar. Before they left him, the boys laid James across the train tracks and weighed his head down with rubble. Two days later, on 14 Sunday February 1993, James Bulger's body was discovered. A passing train had dissected the body. A pathologist later testified that James had died before his body was run over by a goods train.

Thompson and Venables were charged with the murder of James Bulger and had to attend an adult murder trial. A criminal trial generally begins with an appearance at a magistrates court. The Bulger case precipitated a widespread media driven moral panic about the evilness of young people. Thompson and Venables were epitomised as symbols of a dangerous and wicked youth who needed to be locked up. This media frenzy resulted in scenes of public anger, with five hundred angry protesters gathered at South Sefton Magistrates Court for Thomson and Venables' initial court appearances. The boys' parents were moved to different parts of the country and had to assume new identities following a series of death threats. A serious case cannot be heard at the magistrates court, such a case must be heard in a Crown Court by a judge and jury. The full trial of Thompson and Venables took place at Preston Crown Court. Preston Crown Court is a sombre and intimidating Victorian criminal court. The trial was conducted as an adult trial would have been, with the boys sitting in the dock away from their parents and with the judge and court officials dressed in full legal ceremonial dress. Each boy sat in full view of the court on raised chairs (so that they could see out of the dock which was designed for adults) accompanied by two social workers. Although they were separated from their parents, they were within touching distance of them on days that their families attended the trial. News stories frequently reported on the demeanour of the defendants since they were in full view of reporters. From the time of their arrest through the nine months before their trial, Thompson and Venables were held in custody and denied 'treatment in case it prejudiced their pleas' (Penal Affairs Consortium, 1995: 6).

The boys, who offered no evidence in their defence, were found guilty and were sentenced to be detained 'during Her Majesty's pleasure' at a young offender institution. To be incarcerated 'during Her Majesty's pleasure' is an indeterminate sentence which resembles the mandatory life sentence given to adults convicted of murder. A child detained during Her Majesty's pleasure must first serve a minimum period in custody specified in the tariff. The tariff is set at a level intended to reflect the seriousness of the offence and also satisfy society's requirement for retribution and deterrence. Once the tariff has expired the young person will remain in custody until the Parole Board considers that it is safe for them to be released into the community under licence. The licence remains in force for life. If a young person breaches their licence conditions, reoffends or is considered by the youth offending team to pose an enhanced risk to the public then the young person may be returned to custody. The trial judge Justice Morland described the actions of Thompson and Venables as an 'unparalleled evil and barbarity' and told the boys that they would be 'securely detained for very, very many years'. Accordingly he set their minimum period of incarceration at eight years, allowing for a review of the sentence at five years. The trial judge lifted all restrictions on reporting the identities of Thompson and Venables. The sentence was increased on appeal by the then Lord Chief Justice, Lord Taylor of Gosforth, to 10 years with a review after seven years. Both the sentences issued by the trial judge and the Lord Chief Justice would ensure that Thompson and Venable would not serve any part of their sentence in an adult prison. The Criminal Justice Act 1991 allowed the Home Secretary to decide the length of mandatory life sentences. Accordingly the Home Secretary, Michael Howard, raised the minimum sentence to 15 years, with a review after 12 years, on the grounds that he was acting in the public interest. An important feature of this case for Michael Howard was the exceptionally cruel and sadistic nature of the crime, perpetrated against a very young and defenceless victim.

In *R v Secretary of State for the Home Department ex parte Venables and Thompson* ([1997] 3 All ER 97), Thompson and Venables challenged the lawfulness of the Home Secretary's decision to increase their minimum tariff to 15 years on the grounds that he had allowed himself to be influenced by a newspaper campaign and also that as he was a politician he should not be involved in sentencing which is a judicial function. The House of Lords ruled that the Home Secretary could lawfully fix a tariff for young offenders but that in this case the Home Secretary's decision-making was flawed. The House of Lords held that it was inappropriate and unfair for the Home Secretary to consider a petition with 278,300 signatures, a campaign of over 20,000 coupons from *The Sun* newspaper, and over 5,000 letters from the public all demanding that Thomson and Venables should remain in custody for life. The court considered that these were legally irrelevant. The House of Lords held that as the Home Secretary was exercising a power equivalent to a judge's sentencing power he needed to remain detached from the pressure of public opinion. His consideration of public opinion was thus procedurally unfair. The court also held that the Home Secretary had lost sight of the two defendants as immature and had not considered the possibility that Thompson and Venables could develop and progress while in custody. Accordingly the House of Lords quashed the tariff imposed by the Home Secretary.

However Thompson and Venables challenged this decision of the House of Lords in the European court of Human Rights in *V v UK* and *T v UK* ((2000) 30 EHRR 121). The European Court of Human Rights held that the fixing of a tariff by the Home Secretary was contrary to Article 6 of the European Convention on Human Rights. Article 6 protects the right to a fair trial by an independent and impartial tribunal. As the Home Secretary was a member of the government, the European Court of Human Rights ruled that he should not be participating in judicial functions. In October 2000, the Lord Chief Justice, Woolf J, reviewed the case of Thompson and Venables (*Re Thompson and Venables (Tariff Recommendations)* [2001] 1 All ER 737) and fixed their tariff at eight years because of the improvement in their rehabilitation, effectively restoring the original eight-year term. Section 82A of the Powers of Criminal Courts (Sentencing) Act 2000 now requires that the tariff is set by the trial judge and not the Home Secretary. The European Court of Human Rights in *V v UK* and *T v UK* also held that Article 6 had been breached because of the manner in which the trial was conducted. Because of the intense media attention, the public scrutiny and the defendants' 'immaturity and disturbed emotional state', the court considered that Thompson and Venables were unable to participate effectively in the trial.

A criminal prosecution as occurred in the case of Thompson and Venables would be inconceivable in most European countries. According to the Penal Affairs Consortium 'most foreign commentators were amazed that children should be dealt with by an adult-style Crown Court criminal trial (Penal Affairs Consortium, 1995: 6). Many observers questioned whether such young children could comprehend the complexities of a lengthy criminal trial, whether they could cope with the media coverage; whether they actually understood all of the issues and language used in the trial (Penal Affairs Consortium, 1995: 6). As Sereny noted in relation to the trial of Mary Bell and Norma Bell in 1968, a 'jury trial for murder is a fearful matter, deliberately grave in its procedures and awesome in its effect' (Sereny, 1999: 31) and that neither girl had been prepared for the 'solemnity of the courts, for 'two mutually incomprehensible languages' nor for the media, the crowds and the public interest in the case (Sereny, 1999: 71). In 1968 Mary Bell, aged 11 years, and her friend Norma Bell, aged 13 years and no relation, were prosecuted for the murders of two young boys. At their trial at Newcastle Assizes the concept of *doli incapax* was considered as both girls were between 10 and 14 years of age. Mary Bell had grown up in conditions of extreme poverty, abuse and deprivation. The court was given some evidence of the girls' mental state and Mary Bell was convicted of the murders and Norma was acquitted. Mary Bell was detained for 12 years in a variety of hospitals, secure institutions and prisons, including a maximum security prison, and finally released in 1980 when she was 22 years. There was an injunction banning the press from disclosing any details of where she might be living. She changed her name, moved away from Newcastle and later formed a long-term relationship, had a child and has not reoffended in any way since.

## The killing of Silje Raedergard in Norway in 1994

A case similar to the Bulger murder trial proceeded very differently in the Norwegian city of Trondheim. On 15 October 1994 Silje Raedergard was playing with friends on a local football field. She had played with the two boys many times, but this time the game turned rough. While playing snow castles, the two boys became aggressive. They stripped Silje, stoned her and when she fell unconscious they panicked and ran, leaving her to die in the snow. The news of Silje Raedergard's death shocked the small city. With a population of 135,000, the city of Trondheim had only experienced two murders in the six years prior to her death. However, instead of expressing anger and revenge, the local community felt grief and a level of responsibility. The local community felt dismayed that such a thing could happen in their city and felt little anger when the two boys were given counselling for the following four years. The boys' young age meant that the case would be investigated by health and welfare authorities rather than the police. Norwegian law allowed for the boys to have been questioned by a judge in the presence of a lawyer, but only with the express permission of the boys' parents. All of the parents declined to provide consent to this. In Norway the boys were not vilified by the media and labelled evil, they were treated as victims, not killers. The Norwegian press reporting of the Silje Raedergard case expressed compassion for all of the children and families concerned, and attempted to understand the causes of the tragedy and explored ways to prevent future similar incidents. The Norwegian approach contrasted with that of the press reporting of the Bulger case which was sensational, callous and vindictive (Franklin and Petley, 1996: 149).

The legal age for prosecution in Norway stands at 15 (it is 10 years in England and Wales) and so the children were free to return to school within a week of the incident occurring. The parents of the other children accepted this situation and a lot of parents thought that these children needed to be in the school and needed to be taken care of. The names of Raedergard's young assailants were never revealed in the Norwegian press, and neither boy was prosecuted.

---

### Discussion topic

Could the case of Thompson and Venables have been handled in the same way as the Norwegian case?

## Comment

The age of criminal responsibility in England and Wales is 10 years of age which is comparably very low. Thompson and Venables were 10 years old when they killed James Bulger. If the age of criminal responsibility in England was 12 or 14 years, which would be more in line with most European countries, then Thompson and Venables could not have been held criminally responsible for their actions. Alternatively, had Thompson and Venables been nine years of age at the time of the killing, again they could not have been found criminally culpable for the murder of James Bulger. Instead Thompson and Venables would have fallen under the jurisdiction of the Children Act 1989 and the civil Family Proceedings Courts. Thompson and Venables would have been deemed to be either 'children in need' under section 17 of the 1989 Act or children 'at risk of suffering significant harm' under the provisions of section 31 of the 1989 Act. Significantly all proceedings under the Children Act 1989 are governed by the fundamental principle expressed in section 1(1) that 'the child's welfare shall be the courts paramount consideration'. Under section 25 of the Children Act 1989, the local authority has the power to keep a child which it is looking after in secure accommodation. In *Re M (A Child)(Secure Accommodation)* ([2001] 1 FCR 629) the Court of Appeal held that secure accommodation order proceedings under the Children Act is a benign jurisdiction designed to meet the needs of disturbed young people and to inject discipline and structure into their lives.

## Suggested further reading

Cavadino, P. (1996) *Children who kill*, Winchester: Waterside Press.
Haydon, D. and Scraton, P. (2000) '"Condemn a little more: understand a little less": the political context and rights' implications of the domestic and European rulings in the Venables-Thompson case', *Journal of Law and Society*, 27, 3, 416–48.
Rowbotham, J., Stevenson, K. and Pegg, S. (2003) 'Children of misfortune: parallels in the cases of child murderers Thompson and Venables, Barratt and Bradley', *Howard Journal of Criminal Justice*, 42, 2, 107–22.

# Bibliography

Arenella, P. (1990) 'Character, choice and moral agency: the relevance of character to our moral culpability judgements', *Social Philosophy and Policy*, 7, 2, 67.

Aries, P. (1962) *Centuries of Childhood*, Harmondsworth: Penguin.

Arthur, R. (2004) 'Young Offenders: Children in Need of Protection', *Law and Policy*, 26, 3&4, 309–27.

Ashworth, A. (2003) 'Is restorative justice the way forward for criminal justice?', in McLaughlin, E., Fergusson, R., Hughes, G. and Westmarland, L., *Restorative justice: critical issues*, London: Sage.

Asquith, S. (1983) 'Justice, Retribution and Children', in Morris, A. and Giller, H., *Providing Criminal Justice for Children*, London: Edward Arnold.

Audit Commission (1996) *Misspent Youth: Young People and Crime*, London: Audit Commission.

— — (2004) *Youth Justice 2004, A Review of the Reformed Youth Justice System*, London: Audit Commission.

Bainham, A. (2005) *Children: The Modern Law* 3rd edn, Bristol: Family Law.

Bandalli, S. (1998) 'Abolition of the presumption of *doli incapax* and the criminalisation of children', *Howard Journal of Criminal Justice*, 37, 2, 114–23.

— — (2000) 'Children, responsibility and the new youth justice', in Goldson, B. (ed.) *The New Youth Justice*, Lyme Regis: Russell House.

Bateman, T. (2007) 'Youth Rehabilitation Orders to replace all existing community orders', *Youth Justice*, 7, 3, 241–43.

Bedingfield, D. (1998) *The Child in Need: Children, The State and the Law*, Bristol: Family Law.

Berlino, M. and Wansell, G. (1974) *Caught in the Act*, Harmondsworth: Penguin.

Black, T. (2005) 'ASBOs and young people', *The Online Journal of the Law Society of Scotland*, 9 March, www.journalonline.co.uk.

Blackstone, W. (1769) *Blackstone's Commentaries on the Law of England*, Book IV, Chicago: University of Chicago Press.

Bottoms, A. (1974) 'On the decriminalisation of the English juvenile court', in Hood, R. (ed.) *Crime, Criminology and Public Policy*, London: Heinemann.

Bracton, H. de (*c.* 1250) 'De Legibus et Consuetudinibus Angliae', in Woodbine, G. (1910) *Four Thirteenth Century Law Tracts*, Yale: Yale University Press.

Braithwaite, J. (1999) 'Restorative justice: assessing optimistic and pessimistic accounts', *Crime and Justice: A Review of Research*, 25, 1.

Buck, T. (2005) *International Child Law*, London: Routledge.

Campbell, S. (2002) *Implementing Anti-social Behaviour Orders: Messages from Practitioners*, Home Office Findings 160, London: HMSO.

Carlebach, J. (1970) *Caring for children in trouble*, London: Routledge & Kegan Paul.

Carpenter, M. (1853) *Juvenile Delinquents: Social Evils, Their Causes and Their Cure*, London: Cash.

Cavadino, M. and Dignan, J. (1992) *The Penal System: An Introduction*, London: Sage.

— — (2002) *The Penal System: An Introduction*, 3rd edn, London: Sage.

Chakrabarti, S. (2006) 'Blurring the lines between civil and criminal justice', in Shishman, B.(ed.) *Social Justice: Criminal Justice*, London: The Smith Institute.

Chief Inspector of HM Prisons (1999) *HM Young Offenders Institution and Remand Centre Feltham: report of an unannounced full inspection (28–30 September)*, London: HM Inspector of Prisons.

— — (2009) *Report of an unannounced inspection of HMYOI Cookham Wood (2–9 February)*, London: HM Inspector of Prisons.

Chief Secretary to the Treasury (2003) *Every Child Matters*, Cm 5860, London: HMSO.

Collins, D.M. (2001) 'Anti-Social Behavioural Orders – A New False Dawn', *New Law Journal*, 15 June, 876.

Commission on Families and Wellbeing of Children (2005) *Families and the State: Two-way support and responsibilities. An inquiry into the relationship between the State and the Family in the upbringing of children*, London: Policy Press.

Council of Europe (2004) *Space 1, Council of Europe Annual Penal Statistics, Survey 2004*, Strasbourg: Council of Europe.

Crawford, A. and Newburn, T. (2003) *Youth Offending and Restorative Justice: Implementing reform in youth justice*, Devon: Willan.

Cunneen, C. and White, R. (1995) *Juvenile Justice: An Australian Perspective*, Oxford: Oxford University Press.

Department for Education and Skills (2006) *Working together to safeguard children: a guide to inter-agency working to safeguard and promote the welfare of children*, London: The Stationery Office.

— — (2008) *Children Act 1989 Guidance and Regulations Vol. 1: Court Orders*, London: The Stationery Office.

Department of Health (1991) *The Children Act 1989 Guidance and Regulations Vol. 2: Family Support, Day Care and Educational Provision for Young Children*, London: HMSO.

Dignan, J. (1999) 'The Crime and Disorder Act and the Prospects for Restorative Justice', *Criminal Law Review*, 48–60.

Donoghue, J. (2007) 'The judiciary as a primary definer on Anti-Social Behaviour Orders', *Howard Journal of Criminal Justice*, 46, 4, 417–30.

Downes, D. and Hansen, K. (2006) 'Welfare and punishment in comparative perspective' in Armstrong, S. and McAra, L. (eds), *Perspectives on Punishment: The Contours of Control*, Oxford: Oxford University Press.

Eekelaar, J. (2002) 'Beyond the welfare principle', *Child and Family Law Quarterly*, 14, 3, 237.

European Commission (2005) *Report by Mr Alvarao Gil-Robles Commissioner for Human Rights on his visit to the UK*, Geneva: European Commission.

Evans, R. and Puech, K. (2001) 'Reprimands and warnings: populist punitiveness or restorative justice?', *Criminal Law Review*, 794–805.

Fergusson, R. (2002) 'Making Sense of the Melting Pot: Multiple Discourses in Youth Justice Policy', *Youth Justice*, 7, 3, 179–94.

—— (2007) 'Making Sense of the Melting Pot: Multiple Discourses in Youth Justice Policy', *Youth Justice*, 7, 3, 179–94.

Field, S. (2007) 'Practice Cultures and the "New" Youth Justice in (England and) Wales', *British Journal of Criminology*, 47, 311–30.

Fionda, J. (1999) 'New Labour, Old Hat: Youth Justice and the Crime and Disorder Act 1998', *Criminal Law Review*, 46.

Fox, D., Dhami, M.K. and Mantle, G. (2006) 'Restorative Final Warnings: Policy and Practice', *Howard Journal of Criminal Justice*, 45, 2, 129–40.

Fox, S.J. (1996) 'The early history of the Court', *Future of Children*, 6(3): 31–35.

Franklin, B. and Petley, J. (1996) 'Killing the age of innocence: newspaper reporting of the death of James Bulger', in Pilcher, J. and Wagg, S. (eds) *Thatcher's Children?*, London: Falmer.

Gelsthorpe, L. and Morris, A. (1999) 'Much ado about nothing – a critical comment on key provisions relating to children in the Crime and Disorder Act 1998', *Child and Family Law Quarterly*, 11, 3, 209.

Ghate, D. and Ramella, M. (2002) *Positive Parenting: The National Evaluation of the Youth Justice Board's Parenting Programme*, London: Youth Justice Board.

Gil-Robles, A. (2005) *Report by the Commissioner for Human Rights on his visit to the UK*, Strasbourg: Council of Europe.

Glover, J. and Hibbert, P. (2009) *Locking up or giving up – why custody thresholds for teenagers aged 12, 13 and 14 need to be raised*, Essex: Barnardo's.

Goldson, B. (ed.) (2000a) *The New Youth Justice*, London: Russell House.

Goldson, B. (2000b) 'Whither Diversion? Interventionism and the New Youth Justice', in Goldson, B. (ed.) *The New Youth Justice*, Lyme Regis: Russell House.

—— (2005) 'Child imprisonment: a case for abolition', *Youth Justice*, 5, 77.

—— (2006) 'Penal custody: intolerance, irrationality and indifference', in Goldson, B. and Muncie, J., *Youth Crime and Justice*, London: Sage.

Goldson, B. and Jamieson, J. (2002) 'Youth crime, the "parenting deficit" and state intervention: a contextual critique', *Youth Justice*, 2, 2.

Goldson, B. and Muncie, J. (2006) *Youth Crime and Justice: Critical Issues*, London: Sage.

Goldson, B. and Peters, E. (2000) *Tough justice, responding to children in trouble*, London: Children's Society.

Gray, P. (2005) 'The Politics of Risk and Young Offenders' Experiences of Social Exclusion and Restorative Justice', *British Journal of Criminology*, 45, 6, 938–57.

Hagell, A. and Hazel, N. (2001) 'Macro and micro patterns in the development of secure custodial institutions for serious and persistent young offenders in England and Wales', *Youth Justice*, 1, 1, 3–16.

Haines, K. and O'Mahony, D. (2006) 'Restorative approaches, young people and youth justice', in Goldson, B. and Muncie, J. (eds) *Youth Crime and Justice: Critical Issues*, London: Sage, pp. 110–24.

Hale, M. (1736) *Historia Placitorum Coronae*, London: Nutt & Gosling.

Harris, R. (1991) 'The Life and Death of the Care Order (Criminal)', *British Journal of Social Work*, 21, 1–17.

Hayes, M. (1999) 'Offending Behaviour and Children Under 10', *Family Law*, May, 317.

Hine, J. (2007) 'Young people's perspective on final warnings', *Web Journal of Current Legal Issues*, 2.

Hodgkinson, S. and Tilley, N. (2007) 'Policing Anti-Social Behaviour: Constraints, Dilemmas and Opportunities', *Howard Journal of Criminal Justice*, 46, 4, 385–400.

Hollingsworth, K. (2007a) 'Judicial approaches to children's rights in youth crime', *Child and Family Law Quarterly*, 19, 1, 42.

— — (2007b) 'Responsibility and Rights: Children and their Parents in the Youth Justice System', *International Journal of Law, Policy and the Family*, 21, 2, 190–219.

Holt, A. (2008) 'Room for resistance? Parenting orders, disciplinary power and the production of the "bad parent"', in Squires, P. (ed.) *ASBO Nation: the criminalisation of nuisance*, Bristol: Policy Press.

— —, (2009) '(En)Gendering Responsiblities: Experiences of Parenting a "Young Offender"', *Howard Journal of Criminal Justice*, 48, 4, 344–56.

Home Office (1927) *Report of the Departmental Committee on the Treatment of Young Offenders*, London: HMSO.

— — (1946) *The Care of Children*, London: HMSO.

— — (1960) *Report on the Committee on Children and Young Persons*, London: HMSO.

— — (1990) *Crime, Justice and Protecting the Public*, London: The Stationery Office.

— — (1997a) *No More Excuses: A New Approach to Tackling Youth Crime in England and Wales*, London: The Stationery Office.

— — (1997b) *Tackling Youth Crime*, London: The Stationery Office.

— — (1998a) *Youth Justice: Preventing Offending*, London: The Stationery Office.

— — (1998b) *Draft Guidance Document: Anti-Social Behaviour Orders*, London: Home Office.

— — (1999) *Antisocial Behaviour Orders: Guidance*, London: Home Office.

— — (2000) *The Final Warning Scheme – Guidance for Youth Offending Teams*, London: Home Office.

— — (2001) *Local Child Curfew: Guidance Documents: Working Draft*, London: Home Office.

— — (2003) *Youth Justice – the Next Steps*, London: Home Office.

— — (2006) 'The Reprimanding/Warning of Offenders', *Home Office Circular 14/2006*, London: Home Office.

Home Office, Department of Health, Welsh Office, Department for Education and Employment (1998) *Inter-departmental Circular on Establishing Youth Offending Teams*, London: Home Office.

Home Office, Youth Justice Board (2002) *Final Warning Scheme: Guidance for the Police and Youth Offending Teams*, London: Home Office.

Howard, C. (1982) *Criminal Law*, 4th edn, Sydney: Law Book Company.

Howard League (2001) *Children in prison: provision and practice at Castington*, London: Howard League.

Inspector of Prisons (1836) 'First Report of the Inspector of Prisons', *Parliamentary Papers (1836)*, 117, 35, 269.

— — (1838) 'First Report of the Inspector of Prisons', *Parliamentary Papers (1837–38)*, 30, 1.

Kemp, V., Soroby, A., Liddle, M. and Merrington, S. (2002) *Assessing responses to youth offending in Northamptonshire*, London: NACRO.

Kilbrandon, Lord (1964) *Report of the Committee on Children and Young Persons*, Edinburgh: HMSO.

King, M. (1997) *A Better World for Children: Explorations in Morality and Authority*, London: Routledge.

Littlechild, R. (1998) 'An end to "inappropriate adults"?', *Childright*, 8, 8–9.

Lord Chancellor's Department, Crown Prosecution Service, Home Office (1999) *Criminal Justice: Working Together*, London: Stationery Office.

Mack, J.W. (1909) 'The Juvenile Court', *Harvard Law Review*, 23, 104–7.

Major, J. (1993) *Mail on Sunday*, 21 February, p. 8.

Manton, J. (1976) *Mary Carpenter and the Children of the Streets*, London: Heinemann.

Margo, J. and Stevens, A. (2008) *Make me a criminal: preventing youth crime*, London: Institute of Public Policy Research.

Marshall, T.F. (1999) *Restorative justice: an overview*, London: Home Office.

Mason, P. and Prior, D. (2008) 'The Children's Fund and the prevention of crime and anti-social behaviour', *Criminology and Criminal Justice*, 8, 3, 279–96.

McClintock, F. (1963) *Crimes of Violence*, London: Macmillan.

McGhee, J. and Waterhouse, L. (2007) 'Classification in youth justice and child welfare: in search of "the child"', *Youth Justice*, 7, 2, 107–20.

Mennell, R.M. (1973) *Thorns and Thistles: Juvenile Delinquents in the United States 1825–1940*, Hanover: United Press of New England.

Miller, J. (1991) *Last one over the wall: the Massachusetts experiment in closing reform school*, Ohio: Ohio University Press.

Moore, M.S. (1990) 'Choice, character and excuse', *Social Philosophy and Policy*, 7, 2, 29.

Moore, S.A. and Mitchell, R. (2009) 'Rights based restorative justice: evaluating compliance with international standards', *Youth Justice*, 9, 1, 27–43.

Morgan, R. (2007) 'Children and Young Persons', in Jewkes, Y. (ed.) *Handbook on Prisons*, Cullompton: Willan.

Morris, A. (2002) 'Critiquing the critics: a brief response to critics of restorative justice', *British Journal of Criminology*, 42, 3, 596–615.

Morris, A. and Giller, H. (1987) *Understanding Juvenile Justice*, London: Croom Helm.

Muncie, J. (1999) *Youth and Crime – A Critical Introduction*, London: Sage.

— — (2002) 'A new deal for youth? Early intervention and correctionalism', in Hughes, G., McLaughlin, E. and Muncie, J. (eds), *Crime Prevention and Community Safety: New Directions*, London: Sage.

— — (2004) *Youth and Crime*, 2nd edn, London: Sage.

— — (2005) 'The globalization of crime control – the case of youth and juvenile justice: Neo-liberalism, policy convergence and international conventions', *Theoretical Criminology*, 9, 1, 35–64.

— — (2007) 'Youth Justice and the Governance of Young People: Global, International, National and Local Contexts', in Venkatesh, S.A. and Kassimir, R. (eds) *Youth, Globalization, and the Law*, California: Stanford University Press.

NACRO (2000a) *Final Warnings – Implementation Issues. NACRO Briefing June 2000*, London: NACRO.

— — (2000b) *The detention and training order – NACRO briefing*, London: NACRO.

— — (2003) *Pre-Sentence Reports for Young People: A Good Practice Guide*, 2nd edn, London: NACRO.

— — (2006) *The dangerousness provisions of the Criminal Justice Act 2003 and subsequent case law*, NACRO, London.

NCH Scotland (2004) *Where's Kilbrandon Now? Report and Recommendations from the Inquiry*, Glasgow: NCH Scotland.

Newburn, T. (1997) 'Youth, Crime and Justice', in Maguire, M., Morgan, R. and Reiner, R. (eds) *The Oxford Handbook of Criminology*, 2nd edn, Oxford: Oxford University Press.

Newburn, T., Crawford, A., Earle, R., Goldie, S., Hale, C., Hallam, A., Masters, G., Netten, A., Saunders, R., Sharpe, K. and Uglow, S. (2002) *The Introduction of Referral Orders into the Youth Justice System: Final Report*, London: Home Office Research, Development and Statistics Directorate.

O'Donnell, I. and Edgar, K. (1996) *Victimisation in prisons: Home Office Research Findings 37*, London: Home Office.

Penal Affairs Consortium (1995) *The Doctrine of 'Doli Incapax'*, London: Penal Affairs Consortium.

Pitts, J. (2001) *The New Politics of Youth Crime*, Basingstoke: Palgrave.

Radzinowicz, L. and Hood, R. (1990) *The Emergence of Penal Policy in Victorian and Edwardian England*, Oxford: Oxford University Press.

Reece, H. (1996), 'The paramountcy principle: Consensus or Construct?', *Current Legal Problems*, 267.

Rethinking Crime and Punishment and Children's Rights Alliance for England (2002) *Rethinking Child Imprisonment: A Report on Young Offenders Institutions*, London: Children's Rights Alliance.

Richardson, G.D. (1997) 'Restorative justice: framework for the future of corrections', *Corrections Today*, 59, 7, 20–21.

Ruggles-Brise, E.J. (1921) *The English Prison System*, London: Macmillan.

Rutherford, A. (1998) 'A Bill to be Tough on Crime', *New Law Journal*, 9 June, 13.

Rutter, M. and Giller, H. (1983) *Juvenile Delinquency: trends and perspectives*, London: Penguin.

Scott, S. (1907–08) *Senate Debates*, 1044.

Scott, S., O'Connor, T. and Futh, A. (2006) *What makes parenting programmes work in disadvantaged areas?*, York: Joseph Rowntree Foundation.

Scraton, P. and Haydon, D. (2002) 'Challenging the Criminalisation of Children and Young People: Securing a Rights-based Agenda', in Muncie, J., Hughes, G. and McLaughlin, E. *Youth Justice Critical Readings*, London: Sage.

Sereny, G. (1999) *Cries Unheard: the story of Mary Bell*, London: Macmillan.

Simon, J. (2001) 'Entitlement to cruelty: neo-liberalism and the punitive mentality in the United States', in Stenson, K. and Sullivan, R. (eds) *Crime, Risk and Justice*, Cullompton: Willan.

Smith, A. (1994) '*Doli incapax* under threat', *Cambridge Law Journal*, 426.

Smith, R. (2006) 'Actuarialism and Early Intervention in Contemporary Youth Justice', in Goldson, B. and Muncie, J. (eds) *Youth Crime and Justice*, London: Sage.

— — (2007) *Youth Justice: Ideas, Policy, Practice*, Cullompton: Willan.

Social Exclusion Unit (2002) *Reducing reoffending by ex-prisoners*, London: Social Exclusion Unit.

Solomon, E. and Garside, R. (2008) *Ten years of Labour's youth justice reforms: an independent audit*, London: Centre for Crime and Justice Studies.

Stone, N. (2001) 'Custodial sentences: aims and principles in youth justice, disparity and other complexities', *Youth Justice*, 1, 42.

Sutherland, A. (2009) 'The Scaled Approach in Youth Justice: Fools Rush In . . . ', *Youth Justice*, 9, 1, 44–60.

Templewood (1948) *Parliamentary Debates*, H.L. Deb. Vol. 1957, col. 39.

Turner, A. (2007) 'The Criminal Justice Merry-Go-Round', *Justice of the Peace*, 171, 729.

Turner, J. (1958) *Outlines of Criminal Law*, 17th edn, Cambridge: Cambridge University Press.

United Kingdom Children's Commissioners (2008) *Report to the United Nations Committee on the Rights of the Child*, www.11MILLION.org.uk.

United Kingdom Government (1999) *Convention on the Rights of the Child: Second Periodic Report to the UN Committee on the Rights of the Child by the United Kingdom*, Nottingham: Department for Children, Schools and Families.

United Nations Committee on the Rights of the Child (2002) *Consideration of Reports Submitted by State Parties under Article 44 of the Convention. Concluding observations: United Kingdom of Great Britain and Northern Ireland*, CRC/C/15/Add.188, Geneva: Committee on the Rights of the Child.

— — (2007) *General Comment No. 10: Children's Rights in Juvenile Justice*, CRC/C/GC/10, Vienna: UNCRC.

— — (2008) *Consideration of Reports Submitted by State Parties Under Article 44 of the Convention. Concluding observations: Great Britain and Northern Ireland*, CRC/C/GBR/CO/4, Geneva: Committee on the Rights of the Child.

United Nations Office of Drugs and Crime (2006) *Handbook of restorative justice programmes: criminal justice handbook series*, Vienna: United Nations.

United Nations Secretary General (2006) *Report of the Independent Expert for the United Nations Study on Violence Against Children*, A/6199, Geneva: United Nations.

United States Government (1967) *President's Commission on Law Enforcement and Administration of Justice: Task force report*, Washington: U. S. Govt. Print. Off.

Van Beuren, G. (1992) 'Child Oriented Justice – An International Challenge to Europe', *International Journal of Law, Policy and the Family*, 6, 3, 381–99.

Vaughan, B. (2000) 'The Government of Youth: Disorder and Dependence', *Social and Legal Studies*, 9, 3, 347.

Walker, N. (1999) *Aggravation, Mitigation and Mercy in English Criminal Justice*, London: Blackstone.

Weijers, I. (1999) 'The double paradox of juvenile justice', *European Journal on Criminal Policy and Research*, 7, 3, 329–51.

West, D.J (1982). *Delinquency: Its Roots, Careers and Prospects*, London: Heinemann.

Whyte, B. (2003) 'Young and Persistent: Recent Developments in Youth Justice Policy and Practice in Scotland', *Youth Justice*, 3, 74–85.

— — (2009) 'Youth "In Justice" in the UK – which way for Scotland', *Howard Journal of Criminal Justice*, 48, 2, 200.

Wiles, P., Holdaway, S., Marsh, R., Hammersley, R., Dignan, J., Davidson, N. and Hine, J. (1999) *Interim evaluation of Youth Offending Teams*, Sheffield and Hull: Sheffield University and Hull University.

Williams, B. (2001) 'Reparation orders for young offenders: coerced apology?', *Relational Justice*, 9, 8.

Williams, G. (1954) 'The Criminal Responsibility of Children', *Criminal Law Review* 493.

Willow, C. (2005) 'ASBO's: not meeting children's needs', *Howard League Magazine*, 1, 7–8.

Youth Justice Board (2000) 'Detention and training order – a better sentence for young offenders', *Youth Justice Board News*, June.

—— (2002a) *Corporate Plan 2002–03 to 2004–05 and Business Plan 2002–03*, London: Youth Justice Board.

—— (2002b) *Draft National Standards for Youth Justice*, London: Youth Justice Board.

—— (2007) *Youth Justice: The Scaled Approach*, London: Youth Justice Board.

—— (2008a) *Youth Justice Board Guidance*, www.yjb.gov.uk/en-gb/practitioners/CourtsAndOrders/CriminalJusticeandImmigrationAct/

—— (2008b) *Corporate Plan 2008–11, Business Plan 2008/09: Supporting Young People, Making Communities Safer*, London: Youth Justice Board.

# Index